'A Gaggle of Geese', by Alice Taylor

About Alice Taylor:

'one of our best-loved writers ... encourages us all
to treasure what we have' *RTE1's Today Show*

'much-loved Irish author' *Belfast Telegraph*

'one of the country's most accomplished storytellers'
Irish Mail on Sunday

'Ireland's Laurie Lee' *The Observer*

'...Taylor's remarkable gift of elevating the ordinary to something
special, something poetic ...' *Irish Independent*

For more books by Alice Taylor, see www.obrien.ie

Alice Taylor grew up on a family farm near the Cork–Kerry border where life moved at a slow pace. Then over the following years, life in Ireland and Alice's own life accelerated, as she moved to West Cork and became a busy mother and part of an extended family business. Now with the passing of the years she has slowed down, with fewer responsibilities and more time to herself. During the pandemic she witnessed the lifestyle in Ireland forced back almost to the easy pace of her early years.

Other books by Alice Taylor:

To School through the Fields
A Cocoon with a View
Books from the Attic
As Time Goes By
And Life Lights Up
The Women
Do You Remember?
Tea and Talk

See the O'Brien Press website,
www.obrien.ie,
for a full list

Learning from the Elders

*We first witness the realities of growing older
through our grandparents and then our parents.
We also learn as we see elderly
family, friends and neighbours
come to terms with it.
Then it is our turn. Life turns full circle.
I am now very grateful to these family elders and also
to a retired lady who in her later years came to stay
with us and was an example of how to handle the
oncoming tide of years as she skilfully
manipulated her boat through
the challenging, choppy waters.
To all these mentors I am very grateful
as they taught me many things.*

As Time Goes By

Grow old along with me,
The best is yet to be,
The last of life for which the first was made ...

Robert Browning

My early years in Innishannon were a whirlwind. Surrounded by small children, running a guest house, post office and a busy shop, sometimes with much-loved elderly relatives on board, the days were a stampede of non-stop activity. My wonderful husband Gabriel began work at 6am and often balanced the books in the small hours, while at the same time being part of every parish organisation. He kept so many balls in the air that one got dizzy just looking on. We also seemed to be endlessly build-ing and extending the business, and the bank manager was forever threatening to pull the mat from under us so we were constantly over-stretched and stressed.

Sometimes, back then, I would dream of a day away from it all on a desert island where one could only hear 'lake water lapping with low sounds by the shore' ... and then a waiter would magically appear bearing a tray laden with the most gorgeous food, and whip out a starched white linen tablecloth and arrange everything on a low table beside me, and then disappear into the mist. Later, sipping a Gaelic coffee, I would watch the moon rise.

Or I might dream of a day child-free and money-rich when I would drift through exclusive shops, spoilt for choice, and at midday take time out to dine in a top-class restaurant and enjoy the most delicious lunch, finishing up (again) with a Gaelic coffee (I had just mastered the art of making these, following a recipe on a tea-towel bought in a little shop down our street; Gaelic coffee signified real luxury for me back then). I wonder had GB Shaw the likes of me in mind when he wrote: 'Youth is wasted on the young.'

During those frantic times an older lady came to stay with us – or, rather, moved into a tiny upstairs apartment which we had ironically christened the 'West Wing'. She was very elderly (at least to me at the time) and so very posh that we never got to first-name terms; such a thing would be akin to calling the Queen of England 'Lizzy', and such familiarity could not be condoned. Anyway, her name was unpronounceable to me, so she became Mrs C, though it might more appropriately have been Lady C as she had originated in an aristocratic rookery in the West of Ireland. Having lived a varied and interesting life all over the world, she was a wise old owl and I learned a lot from her, though at first I wondered how she came to be slumming it with the likes of us. 'The old should surround themselves with the young,' she informed me, which explained why she had landed herself in our midst.

One day I was running up the stairs dragging a basket of laundry with me while she waited at the top, leaning on her black ebony walking stick before beginning her painfully slow descent. On my arrival at the top she imperiously instructed, in her impeccable Anglo-Irish accent, 'Alice, my dear, don't ever grow old. It's an appalling condition!'

To me at the time her conditions didn't look half bad! She had successfully mastered the art of making the most of her life, which undoubtedly was now very different to what she had been accustomed to. Choice pieces of her family's heirlooms had accompanied her into the West Wing, and a Jack Yeats masterpiece, gifted by the artist himself, graced her wall. She regularly wined, dined and played bridge with like-minded friends, while a whiff of cigar smoke and brandy wafted along the corridor and downstairs to us below. At Christmas she went to Harrods to do her shopping. Not a bad life in any man's language. Certainly not to me at that time.

But now when I wake up in the morning, checking if all my parts are still functioning and capable of getting me onto the floor, and then how fast they will get me to my required destination, at the same time steadying myself in case I go head first into that destination – then I remember her. On top of the same stairs when I grasp the hand-rail and steady my pace to carefully make my way down in the hope of a safe landing – then I remember, and agree with her. And now in the garden when attempting to lift a heavy pot and my back tells my head that that I have stooped too low – then I remember and salute her. Despite her opinion that old age was appalling, she nevertheless had nurtured the art of coping admirably with it. And though unaware of it at the time, I learned a lot from her. As an old nun at school used to tell us: 'Sound is heard, but example thunders.'

At that time, Gabriel and I loved to dance and, on hearing a favourite tune on the radio, would take off in an energising quick-step around the kitchen table. Now I grasp the brush handle and do a graceful glide into a slow waltz. My pace has certainly slowed down as life changed over the years, from being part of a large family, to half of a couple, and now a solo player.

Some people are home alone by choice, while others, like myself, evolved into it through a change of circumstances. But no matter how it comes about, living alone has its minuses and its pluses, and as the years go by you strive to get the balance right. You slowly grow accustomed to being on your own and you adjust to enjoying your own company and keeping yourself pleasantly occupied.

And then, to really test our mettle and coping skills, along came Covid-19, creeping in like a thief in the night and challenging medical expertise, the world economy, and the resilience of us all. At first we thought that it would be short-term and that soon all would be well again. But then the realisation slowly dawned that this was not just a skirmish but a war, and that we could not afford to get battle-weary because this silent enemy was deadly and persistent, so we would all have to dig deep and nurture long-term coping strategies and greater resilience.

Normally, living alone can be challenging, but there is a much deeper aloneness with Covid as it has cut away our social fabric, and you really miss pleasant outings and the company of friends, and neighbours popping in and out. And in this new aloneness you are more aware too that this is not the time to slip on a banana skin or topple off a step-ladder and end up in A&E. Because not only might there be nobody around to pick up the pieces, there might be nobody around either to provide transport in the event of such a calamity. And hospital was not exactly the place you wanted to be in these times, and, to put the tin hat on it, if you did finish up there you could be isolated for your own safety and not see the familiar face of a visitor for your entire stay. This alerts you to a new need to be more careful in case you come a cropper.

I remember Mrs C more often now and think how wise she was to move in with us because the young certainly do energise and entertain. She invited our children up to her West Wing (at specified times) to teach them how to play bridge and to put manners on them. I wonder how she would have coped with the different lockdown levels which we seem to be in and out of now like the cuckoo in a cuckoo clock. Pretty well, one would imagine. She was very resourceful and not into complaining. She had the resilience of one who had experienced the ups and downs of life, and she was certainly not obsessed with her own pains and aches, though undoubtedly at her age they must have been part of the package. One day when I enquired why she never complained, she told me, 'My mother gave me one very valuable bit of advice: "Gundred, she told me, never complain, it destroys yourself and annihilates people."' So she never did. She kept herself well occupied and mentally alert with reading, doing crosswords, watching and listening to all kinds of sports on radio and TV, reading *The Times* daily and keeping up-to-date with world events, and she also had a great interest in what was going on locally, even in the smallest details. One evening as we chatted while looking down at the pub across the road, an elderly lady and her slightly doddery male companion went in and would be there, we knew, until well after closing time. This odd couple had recently moved in together, which caused Mrs C to wryly comment, 'What a strange relationship that is, I doubt that she has him for his sexual prowess.' She had a wicked sense of humour and would often articulate something that one might be thinking but would not like to verbalise. She always wanted to know what was going on downstairs and in the village. And every night before retiring she indulged herself and enjoyed a large hot whiskey.

The monks living in isolation on Skellig Michael, who have always fascinated me, had no such comforts and one would have to wonder how on earth they survived in that bleak, lonely, desolate place with none of the comforts of life that we have. Did isolation unearth and release creativity and resilience? Could that resilience and creativity lie deep down in the unplumbed depths of us all, I wonder? Is there something to be learned from this strange, weird world into which we had all been thrust? At my stage of life I thought that I had seen it all, but this was a whole new sobering experience. And then, on my eighty-third birthday came a card from my daughter of a formidable-looking lady wearing a 'don't mess with me expression' and arms purposefully folded across a well upholstered bosom, with a quote beneath it from the legendary Bette Davis: 'Old age ain't no place for sissies.' Could this isolation as well as the ageing process be a learning curve?

What I began to learn was that the strategies needed to cope with the isolation of Covid-19 and those needed to cope with living alone and growing older are often fairly similar – being absorbed in doing: painting, reading, creating, gardening and so on. When you no longer run a family or a business or go out to work, these enjoyable pursuits can become your focus. And isn't it great to have the time to savour them?

Maybe now too could be the time to remember a poem that was in my mind of a long-held belief that slowing down and living in harmony with nature enriches your life. This awareness was seeded during childhood on the home farm, and over the years grew with me. Then very early one morning, while sitting alone in my sister's wild garden in Toronto watching the sun rise and listening to the dawn chorus, the poem sprouted in my mind – probably triggered by the magic of the sunrise and the birdsong but also by a childhood image of going out in the early-morning dew to round up the cows for milking. The cows at that time of the morning were all lying down around the field, peacefully chewing the cud and they had no wish to be disturbed from their bovine meditation. Cows have no concept of hurry and will never engage in it unless stampeded into it by us hurrying humans, and even then it is totally unacceptable to them as their body is not designed for speed. So their first reaction on being alerted to the prospect of disturbing themselves is to slowly ease into their own body and check out their readiness to cope with any proposed movement. Cows are full of awareness, and are in complete harmony with the sun as it slowly rises above the horizon alerting the birds – then one bird awakens with a faint twitter and very gently others join in, and slowly the volume rises until finally the whole chorus are all in full song. But this is all done slowly and gently. Nature can teach us so much.

Unfold Me Gently
Unfold me gently
Into this new day,
As the sun slowly
Edges the horizon
Before bursting into
A dazzling dawn;
As the birds softly

Welcome the light
Before breaking into
A full dawn chorus;
As the cow rises
And stretches into
Her own full body
Before bellowing
To her companions –

May I too slowly absorb,
Be calmed and centred
By the unfolding depths
Of this bright new day
So that my inner being
Will dance in harmony
With whatever
It may bring.

Solitude...

When you live on your own
you savour precious moments.
And you select projects and occupations that you
find truly absorbing, activities that for years you
may have put on hold,
like writing, painting, reading and gardening.
You also have the time to improve your ability to
do things at which you were previously
not very good.
For years I had envied good gardeners, artists and
knitters, and now I am attempting to improve at all
these absorbing hobbies. Learning new skills is also
a challenge. For someone interested in wildlife and
gardening, for example, perfecting the arts
of photography or flower arranging
can be uplifting and engaging experiences.
All these activities help to keep
the mind exercised and alive.

Let's Have a Cup of Tea

A re-awakening had taken place! A discerning friend brought me a packet of loose tea from Ballymaloe. But I was so carried away with the other item in the packet that she was long gone before I became aware of the little cellophane-wrapped bag of black tea. My mind had been totally focused on the pot of Ballymaloe raspberry jam. Knowing from experience how wonderful this raspberry jam was, the very sight of it stimulated my taste buds. This jam deserved an appreciative reception. So it was first held up to the light of the window to better admire its depth and richness of colour. The contents were the final crescendo of a fruit harvest that had absorbed the warmth of the sun, the kiss of the rain, the touch of the buzzing bees and the softness of balmy country air – and all that goodness was now resting in this potful of glowing raspberries. My much-appreciated pot of jam was placed lovingly on the dresser shelf from where its deep glow enhanced the colour palette of its surroundings.

When I had finally finished paying homage to the jam, my eye fell on the little bag of tea proclaiming itself to be

Ballymaloe Morning Tea. Broody, black and full of hidden eastern mystery, this little bag of loose tea had found its way unknowingly into dangerously unappreciative territory. Because this house is common tea-bag terrain.

Though reared by a mother who created a ritual out of tea making, I had become a lapsed tea maker. My mother's self-appointed standards never varied and she refused to make tea from any kettle that she herself had not seen come to the boil. Her scalding of the teapot was akin to the preparation of a connoisseur's glass about to receive priceless hot port. Her exactitude about measuring the tea was the result of years dedicated to her art. She was hailed within our family circle as having the skill of making THE perfect cup of tea. But not so her daughter! Not so! At least, not this daughter. Oh, how the mighty had fallen.

But could all this be about to change? As I stood silently gazing at this bag of dark, loose tea, son Number 2 put his head in the door at the other end of the kitchen and looked at my bag of Morning Tea in surprise.

'Well, now, what's all this about?' he enquired in a puzzled voice. 'Are you going back to making real tea?'

'Not sure,' I told him hesitantly, 'but isn't there something nice about the look of this bag of loose tea?'

'Why did you change to tea bags in the first place?' he asked curiously. 'Nana would never have used tea bags.'

'Convenience, I suppose,' I admitted reluctantly.

'But what was more convenient about tea bags?' he questioned.

'No tea leaves, I suppose.' I was remembering out loud rather than answering his question.

'But what's wrong with tea leaves?' he queried.

'I suppose they were a bit of a nuisance in the sink,' I admitted.

'Interesting,' he concluded, and that I assumed was the end of that.

But the following evening he arrived in with a small teapot fitted inside with a little porous basket called an infuser into which you put your tea leaves, and after partaking of the tea you simply lifted out this little infuser and up-ended the contents into the compost bin. Impressive! All of a sudden I was on the road to Damascus. I, who had been a lost soul to proper tea-making, was about to rejoin the fold.

But the return of this prodigal daughter necessitated some changes in the culinary department. Loose tea requires a caddy and this special tea required a classy caddy, and at first I thought that I had none to qualify for the position. Then my eye fell on the answer. On my dresser shelf was a heavy, chunky, navy-blue jar with 'Harrods Food Halls' inscribed in gold calligraphy across its chest. It was a gift from a friend who had visited that elite establishment and had brought me back this jar filled with coffee, and when the contents were consumed, the jar, with its elegant appearance and firm clasp, was too gorgeous be disposed of, so it got a home on the dresser. Empty and useless, but beautiful. A hoarder's temptation. But now, at last, its hour had come. My hoarding was about to be justified. This jar would make the ideal

caddy for my precious tea. Now, before you say it, I know that a jar is not exactly a tea caddy, but this jar was so beautiful and its genealogy so impressive, and the friend who gave it to me so special, that all these credentials qualified it for the caddy position. The next step was a suitable spoon to dispense the tea from this posh jar into my precious pot. And I had the perfect one. Buried amongst the cutlery in the dresser drawer, and also buried in my mental memory drawer, was a silver egg spoon inherited from my mother. It would be the ideal measure and it fitted perfectly into the jar. Now, we know that an egg spoon is not a teaspoon, but it somehow seemed right that my tea-making mother should have an input into these proceedings.

And so, the following morning, for the first time in years, it was back to proper tea. The quality of the tea pouring from my dinky little teapot had a rich, amber glow that I had not seen for a long time. The flavour of my mother's tea was back. Unwittingly over the years, I had cast her expertise aside.

Full of enthusiasm I rang my sister, who had never deviated from tea leaves, to tell her about my re-awakening. 'I was wondering when you would cop yourself on,' she told me unceremoniously.

That afternoon I retrieved some scones from the freezer and popped them into the Aga where they heated back to life while I made tea, adhering to all my mother's well-remembered guidelines. Then I set the tea tray with my best china and carried it out into the garden where I savoured my scones, laden with the gorgeous raspberry jam and accompanied by a perfect cup of tea. My mother's art of tea making had been redeemed and reclaimed. Tea leaves were now back in my life, thanks to my friend, Ide, and to Bally-maloe. A reawakening had taken place.

But a further embellishment to this rediscovered delight was about to be added. A friend, on hearing of my recent acquisition, produced a gorgeous little rich-red knitted tea cosy with a dark green tassel on top, which, when turned inside out, became a silver tea cosy with a smart red bow on top.

This tea cosy was made by an amazing young woman who was born into a resourceful farming family and who, despite being visually impaired since childhood, has mastered an incredible number of life skills. Years previously her creative grandmother and I had painted together and her gifted mother's poems make inspirational reading. So my tea cosy came with an enriching family story attached, which made it very special.

All this caused me to question what other pleasant practices I may have unwittingly abandoned, leaking away life's simple pleasures. Was now the time to revisit some of these enriching rituals that fast-forward living had obliterated?

The Gift of a Book

'Through a chink too wide there comes in no wonder,' wrote the poet Patrick Kavanagh. The stony grey fields of his small Monaghan farm crucified the poet, and yet inspired him to pen some of his most memorable works. To escape the drudgery of this hard farm life he went further afield and maybe felt that in the larger spectrum he lost some of his wonder. There's a saying in Irish that my husband often quoted: *An rud is anamh is iontach*, meaning the rare thing is the most wondrous thing. And my grandmother used to tell us 'What's scarce is wonderful.' So, following that logic, when, for social and economic reasons, books were a scarce commodity in the farmhouses of rural Ireland in the 1940s and 1950s, they were held in the highest esteem. For that reason too, a faded, green hardback copy of *Oliver Twist*, which happened to be in our house, was repeatedly read, and even our schoolbooks were treasured. Any publications coming into the house, such as *Ireland's Own* and the *Reader's Digest*, were absorbed in their entirety and deeply appreciated. And when the County Council opened a library in our town it was like manna in the desert, and then a rare visit to Cork city revealed a display of Emily Brontë and Jane Austen books in Woolworths, each for the

princely sum of one shilling and six pence. This brought paradise within reach.

Maybe that is the reason why every year before Christmas I harvest books like a squirrel collecting nuts for the winter. So this year when Covid stole in like a thief in the night, it was good to have the Christmas nest-egg of books waiting to be savoured.

The bottom shelf of the kitchen dresser has become a home for books particularly enjoyed, books waiting to be enjoyed, or familiar perennials that can be dipped into when the need arises. The needs are many and varied, from the inspiration of special poetry books to be savoured when the spirit moves, or comfort books when feeling sorry for myself. Some people dismiss self-help books, but to me anything that supports me when I need a crutch is more than welcome because in life no matter what dilemma confronts us, the chances are that someone else has already walked in those shoes, and if their experience makes ours more manageable, that is something to be appreciated. I love the Eastern wisdom of 'Hope is like a road in the country where there wasn't ever a road – but when many people walk on it, the road comes into existence.'

No one had walked on the road of Covid-19, so in this strange territory we were all walking in the dark and figuring out for ourselves how best to cope with this tough, challenging scenario. This was extreme solitary living. A good friend constantly reminds me that life is a learning curve, and this Covid curve was certainly teaching us many things, and in the process stretching our stamina to the limit. In testing times we all have our own coping strategies and one of the best must surely be the journey through a good book. Escapism? Without a doubt. Getting stuck into a book is one of the most wonderful enrichments of living alone – the experience is extra rich when there are no distractions around.

Going into a bookshop forearmed with a recommended list can be an interesting voyage, but sometimes it can be more exciting to meander around with no preconceived ideas and pick up and choose by instinct. When you do this, you may wander into very unexpected and dangerous places. Last Christmas I picked up *The Beekeeper of Aleppo*, thinking it would be about a beekeeper, and, because I grew up on a farm with a beekeeping brother who had a lifelong love affair with bees, I have never ceased to be intrigued by the world of beekeeping. So, on reading the title, it was the word 'beekeeper' that registered with me, not 'Aleppo'. And the book was indeed about a beekeeper, but the place where this kind and gentle man was unfortunate enough to do his beekeeping had far more to do with the book than the fact that he was a beekeeper. But it was an amazing book. Though a tough read, it was a stark revelation that opened a window into a terrible world about which I knew very little except what is reported on news bulletins. The story centres on a gentle beekeeper, his artist wife who lost her sight due to the trauma of the terrible scenes she had witnessed, and their little boy who was killed by the military in the brutal struggles in Syria. It was a heart-wrenching read that imprinted on the mind the dreadful reality of the brutal goings-on at the other side of the world. We hear these things reported on the news, but reading a detailed human account hammers them right home. The book made me realise that even though we were experiencing Covid-19 we were still a long way from the suffering going on in other places. We had no war and our government was doing its best to help us cope. Some books take us to harrowing zones into which we might not choose to go, but sometimes they can be a sharp wake-up call and instrumental in lifting us out of complacency.

Then, during lockdown, with the bookshops closed, many of us found ourselves grazing our own bookshelves looking for unread books. Sometimes books belonging to other family members might be in the house for many years before you come around to picking one up to read. This happened to me recently. This book belonged to my sister, Ellen, who was an avid reader, and her books are still on shelves around the house. Though I have read most of them, some are still on the 'to be read' queue. One morning, while meandering aimlessly around the house looking for distraction, I picked up *Ten Poems to Change Your Life* and thought, sceptically, what a highly unlikely possibility that was. Nevertheless, as it was still very early in the morning and I was not in the mood to apply myself to doing anything practical, I returned to bed to explore this book with such a high opinion of itself. With a great sense of scepticism,

I opened the book, wondering why, though it had been in the house over ten years and published over twenty years previously, it had remained unexplored by me for so long. The reason had to be the title. I must have thought that any book with such an arrogant claim was probably puffed up with its own self-importance. So I was too puffed up and arrogant to read it! That made two of us!

But there was nothing pretentious about the cover. It was a very faded pale blue hardback with an image of a plain white jug, on which was inscribed the title of the book. Not a fancy, elegant jug either, but a simple, solid jug with no airs and graces about it. Now, I have a thing about jugs and a lifelong love affair with them, and bearing that in mind it was surprising that this jug had not enticed me over the years into this book. It definitely must have been the title that put me off.

The title and presentation of a book can be a very delicate exchange of emotions. It is often the start of a love affair that can go on for years. So the first tentative steps in this relationship may be a very fragile balance. Most of us have in our lives old books that hold out their comforting pages when the world is too much for us. But most of these are tried and tested, and as you grow older and hopefully a little wiser, you get more discerning about which books you welcome into that sacred space. Would this book become one of them?

So, back into bed went myself, the jug and the ten poems. Two hours later I came up for air, feeling that I had absorbed the mental equivalent of a ten-course dinner without a break. The poets inside in this jug covered a mind-boggling spectrum spanning many centuries and belief systems, beginning with Mary Oliver and concluding with John of the Cross. I had never previously read any of these poets. But it was all too much and too overwhelming, so I felt the need to take a breather and to allow for slower absorption. Back in 1720 Sir Richard Steele had observed: 'Reading is to the mind what exercise is to the body.' And I had just run a marathon. A poem per day was the new plan, and so *Ten Poems to Change Your Life* joined the clutter of books scattered on my bedroom floor around the rocking chair where I hibernate when the comfort of these selected old friends is needed. And so the journey began, and over the following weeks whenever the spirit moved, the jug and I relaxed into the rocking chair and one poem at a time was slowly poured out and absorbed, and on coming to the end, begun again. The simple white jug on the cover was actually an inspired choice because it refilled itself again and again. Did the poems change my life? They certainly gave food for thought and a fresh perspective on the pandemic.

Shortly afterwards, the gift of a book of Emily Dickinson's poems arrived by post: *Hope is the Thing with Feathers*. Don't you love the title, a line taken from one of her poems – so appropriate to the pandemic, I thought. Already up in the attic was an old copy of her *Collected Poems*, first published in 1924, but this lovely latest edition reignited interest, causing the early Emily to be resurrected and both

ten poems
to
change
your life

ROGER HOUSDEN

books enjoyed. She who had spent most of her life in voluntary seclusion, would have had no problem living with our current isolation.

I'm nobody! Who are you?
Are you nobody, too?
Then there's a pair of us – don't tell!
They'd banish us, you know.

How dreary to be somebody!
How public, like a frog
To tell your name the livelong day
To an admiring bog!

Emily Dickinson would certainly never have gone on Facebook.

My Beloved Comforter

Since its wool left the back of a sheep long before reaching the loom, it had not been touched by water. I had loved it too dearly to chance immersing it in water. But now that hour had come! This was its first dipping, so I reminded myself to be very, very *cúramach*, as we say in Irish – painstakingly careful. Over many years this garment and I had developed a deep and loving relationship. Not a flash-in-the-pan whirlwind of passion, as sometimes happens with items of a flashier type, but a deep, long-lasting, tried-and-tested friendship. It came into my life at a time when babies and business had stolen away occasions of self-indulgent dalliances through brilliantly lit shops. But an outing to satisfy all these suppressed longings came about annually when, child-free and with two All-Ireland Final tickets in our pockets, Gabriel and I headed for Croke Park, and always detoured to Kilkenny to visit the Design Centre. This hallowed hall of good-quality creations was the highlight of my weekend – even if Cork were playing in the All-Ireland Final! My love affair with the Kilkenny Design Centre shone like a diamond in an otherwise mundane life.

First came the delightful sighting of the beautiful city, then the walk along the atmospheric streets and finally the door of the Design Centre where the whiff of wool, tweed, linen and leather blended with the aroma of good food floating down from the upstairs realm of culinary delights. This was a new kind of shopping experience in Ireland at that time. Even before putting a hand on any item in this glorious Aladdin's cave of temptation, the anticipated thrill of doing so danced in the mind. All around were shelves laden with the best of Irish crafts: pottery, glassware, table mats, oven gloves, aprons, shawls, rainwear and all kinds of everything.

One year, while I was savouring this delightful display, a tall, arrogant, strident red rooster caught my eye. From his perch on high he seemed to be crowing down at me: I'd look great on top of your kitchen press. And so he would. Instant decision! 'Big Bird, you are coming home to Cork with me.' At the time we were transforming our kitchen from the boring, industrial, built-in necessities of a guest-house kitchen to the more interesting requirements of a family home. With this changeover had come a restored tall oak kitchen press, the top of which would be the ideal perch for this Big Bird. It was made for him. But was I tempting fate? Because the next day Cork were about to take on Kilkenny in the All-Ireland Final and could buying this imperious Kilkenny Big Bird be temping fate? Could he be symbolic of the victorious Kilkenny manager striding across the turf of Croke Park flushed with post-match success? But superstitious forebodings were stifled, and this magnificent male was kidnapped from his high shelf and on his way to a Cork homecoming. He was in the bag, whatever about the match. In subsequent years after All-Ireland Finals, this haughty bird was often eyed balefully when Kilkenny had caused us to sip the bitter taste of defeat by snatching *our* MacCarthy Cup! But he was soon forgiven because, despite the inflicted humiliation, one had to be impressed by his admirable stance and sense of superiority.

But of all the items purchased in the Design Centre over the years, the one that outshone all others was this much-loved jacket, now about to be immersed for the first time in sudsy water. It's hard to explain how it escaped so long without an immersion. Maybe I was influenced by an old weaver of wool who said: 'Wash your jumper, shear your sheep.' Was it too risky to wash it at this stage? But surely natural fibre has the innate ability to encounter and survive the struggles of life, and still look good? Indeed, this jacket had survived remarkably well, but now, a bit like myself, it was a subdued shadow of its former self. This was to be expected after almost half a century of sheltering me from the chills of life. It was what one would have to regard as a treasured friend of whom wise Shakespeare could well have said: 'Those friends thou hast, and their adoption tried, Grapple them unto thy soul with hoops of steel.' But now these hoops of steel were about to be loosened as lockdown was rattling my cage and causing me to cast a critical eye over everything, including this old friend.

On first sighting in the shop, it was reclining gracefully in a glass cabinet where it looked as if a rainbow had filtered in. The colour combination was of a wildflower meadow blended with a bog in bloom. A sighting to render one speechless. I approached the cabinet in awe, sensing that this was a rare moment to be savoured. When the profusion of delicately blended colours was raised out of its gilded cage, the creamy white of the mountain-sheep wool came into focus between the magical colours of the rainbow. It felt like thistledown. It was lined with delicate blue silk and each bone button bore a raised, hand-painted wildflower. It looked divine, felt heavenly and was simply irresistible.

Taking a deep breath, my eye sought the price tag, and admittedly I did gasp a little. But when you are a seldom shopper, you feel justified in an occasional big splurge. And now, long after the price was forgotten, the quality of this beautiful creation was still appreciated. In its early years, as with all costly, classy acquisitions, it was treated with the utmost respect and worn only when the need to impress presented itself. Then, gradually, its outings were increased and it accompanied me to late-night concerts where a chill could creep in. It came to the rescue for night feeds, too, when its comforting arms encompassed both mother and child. Then it travelled to matches when maternal side-line support was required in sometimes bleak and chilly surroundings. And, eventually, it came to book signings where it could be draped over a chair and then drafted into action if one were parked too close to a draughty door. And, eventually, it came out to the garden where on late-night meanderings you were wrapped in its comforting arms. Its most recent resting place was in a little press by the Aga which is the warming cupboard for outdoor woolly socks, hats and gloves. Here it would absorb a gentle heat, and later, when reading or watching TV, I would welcome its woolly warmth.

But this morning the fates and Covid tempted me and before being returned to its usual little bolt-hole this old friend got an appraising look – and a snap decision was made that a warm bath was required. But first it was laid out on the kitchen table for a pre-op inspection. The lining had developed frayed edges and in places departed from the main body and I wondered would my sewing skills stretch to replacement. I am no seamstress, but in lockdown anything is possible. But, apart from the lining, it was in fine nick, with all the original buttons still holding their own. I felt like hugging it in appreciation and singing a serenade. Into my mind drifted a song brought back to our home farm by emigrant prairie men who spent many years in Oregon out sheep-herding, where a special horse became their best friend:

Old Faithful, we rode the hills together
Old Faithful, in every kind of weather
When your round-up days are over
There'll be pastures white with clover
For you, old faithful friend of mine.

So I buttoned up my old friend, gave it a warm parting hug and turned on the taps in the large Belfast sink. Under the gushing water I poured in a shower of washing powder, slushing it around into a frothy, sudsy, warm bath. On first immersion the water went murky brown, and the next immersion was slightly less so. It took four such baths before the water eventually flowed clear. Then two deep rinses and finally into a tray it went to be carried to the spin drier, into which it landed with a heavy, sodden slosh. A few minutes later out it came, pounds lighter and glowing with new life. As I laid it out on the table to soothe its rumpled weave, a tag, previously invisible, came alive: 'Síocháin', hand-loomed in County Wicklow, Ireland. What a pity that the name of the artist and date of creation was not included because this, indeed, was a long-standing monument to the quality of Irish farming, design and creation.

Catch Your Hare

All my life I dreamt of applying paint to canvas, but that opportunity never seemed to come about. However, I never lost sight of the dream and eventually the time came and I took to painting like a duck to water, sometimes with the same results – when a duck hits the water he makes a big splash, and sometimes that is all I succeeded in doing. But it is so important in life to 'hold fast to dreams because if dreams die life is a broken-winged bird that cannot fly.'

At the top of our stairs is a room which in recent years got rechristened the 'art room'. This new name was more an act of hope than the possibility of achievement. The art room has two doors into the corridor. This is due to the fact that in our guest-house days this room was actually two bedrooms and at the time of conversion there seemed to be no good reason to remove the second door, a decision taken due more to lack of funding than foresight. But time proved that it was a good decision because directly opposite each door is a window looking over the village street and straight across at Dromkeen wood. So now as you walk along the corridor and look in through the open doors you catch glimpses of the wood in its different seasonal coats.

Having begun my painting efforts in the corner of the kitchen, where you pollute the air with the smells of paints and oils, and from where you are constantly required to either tidy yourself up or be evicted, it was a great relief to retreat to this haven of undisturbed tranquility. Up here, it was possible to spread out in comfort without having the threat of eviction constantly hanging over your head. One son, handy with a hammer, shelved the high gable-end wall, and books from all corners of the house quietly moved in, and slowly, over the years, the art room gradually transformed itself into a library as well. Due to their silent, soothing presence, books are the ideal stable companions and when the frustration of artistic blockages arise they offer the ideal option of a calming peruse along the shelves. Having selected an old friend as a soothing companion, you can then take to the rocking chair inside the window and gently rock yourself into the peaceful waters of escapism. Hiding in different corners of the room are painting disasters and on display is the odd canvas that can to be viewed without a cringe.

On first acquiring the luxury of all this space, there was a rush of blood to the head and non-stop production ensued. My rural roots became evident as cows, calves, then pheasants and other birds of all shapes and plumages flew on to the canvases. Scenes of old houses and rusty gates found their way up the stairs and onto the easel, providing hours of endless fascination. My grandmother's long-gone, old, low, thatched house, still in my memory box and in a family photo album, gave hours of endless nostalgic pleasure and brought delight as a special wedding present for one of her great-grandchildren.

But, eventually, this stream of wild euphoria eased and though an occasional painting was produced, gradually the artistic enthusiasm dried up completely, and paints and brushes were abandoned. Then another son while home on holidays declared that the condition of my abandoned paints and brushes was appalling. Though sometimes necessary, no one likes to have the error of their ways pointed out to them. But guilt and common sense prevailed and I viewed the condition of the abandoned tubes, brushes, and palette knives with dismay. A big clean-up ensued, which took two full days, as dislodging hardened paint out of the caps of numerous tubes and sorting out and restoring neglected brushes and palette knives is a slow, laborious business. But eventually everything was restored and ready for action – though, unfortunately, no action ensued. The love affair between me and painting had evaporated.

But then came Covid-19 and all changed, changed utterly – and I would like to echo Yeats and declare that a terrible beauty was born, but that remained to be seen. However, though my passionate love affair with the canvas had faded, there still lurked, like the faded remnants of a long-dead romance, traces of that once vibrant passion. Because over the non-painting years I had often seen something which caused me to think longingly: Wouldn't that make a lovely painting. And it was probably this vestige of a my long-gone painting passion that one day caused me, while out shopping prior to the arrival of the dreaded virus, to pick up a beautiful photograph of a hare taken by a brilliant local photographer. In the photograph you can almost feel this hare vibrating with alert but suppressed energy. At the first sign of danger he is ready to spring into action. What beautiful animals they are and maybe the fact that they are so seldom sighted has created this almost mystical lore around them. One might well wonder do they span the gulf between our world and another world, as in some folklore.

So that hare came home with me and perched for weeks on top of my desk, from where he looked above me into a far-distant place beyond my limited vision. But from his desktop perch, he encompassed me in his wild and wonderful world. Then one day he and I, like two illicit lovers, crept upstairs into the art room and he perched himself on top of the easel. His very stance brought to mind the famous words of Mrs Beeton, she of the British culinary expertise, in her recipe for hare soup when she advises: 'First catch your hare.' What a wise old bird she was, as that was no easy task! The challenge for me now was to catch my hare on canvas. No mean achievement either!

The first mistake I made was to choose too large a canvas. I was thinking big, but on this canvas the hare lost some of his impact. The hare and I struggled for two days and there were moments when I thought that I had him, but then he disappeared into the mists. He was proving to be elusive and frustrating. But that is painting! It can be a journey through agony to ecstasy – but this was all agony. This hare was refusing to dance with me, and was driving me demented. All thoughts of Covid-19 were eradicated as the hare and I struggled for mastery, but mostly the hare was the victor.

After a week it was time to call a halt. I was not entirely happy with the result but persuaded myself that he could be all right. How wrong can you be? They say that beauty is in the eye of the beholder, but that all depends on the beholder, and this time maybe the beholder was suffering from wishful thinking? So it was time to test the waters. We were on level 3 Covid regulations so my 'bubble' family could drop in. Now, I believe that if you want an honest opinion you ask your children, especially if they are of the male variety. The handy-with-a-hammer son, after a few moments of viewing, decided, 'There is something wrong with his back legs.' I could cheerfully have hit him with his hammer! But undoubtedly he had hit the nail on the head because that doubt was already in my mind, though the last thing that I wanted to hear was a confirmation of my doubts. Then my daughter arrived in with seven-year-old Ellie in tow. My daughter viewed my hare and struggled to let me down gently: 'Mom, are his back legs a bit not quite right?'

'They are all wrong,' her brother confirmed. 'There is the look of a deer about him.'

'You're right!' My daughter was surprised into agreement. 'He does look like a deer.'

But Ellie, seeing my stricken face, came to the rescue. 'Nana, I think that your picture is lovely,' she declared. Thank

heaven for little girls!

But my worst fears had been confirmed. I had certainly not captured the hare. Prior to my consultation with my art reviewers I had had my doubts, and now they were confirmed. The axe had fallen! Time to think it out again! So, back to the drawing board.

The hare had eluded me but could anything be salvaged? Back came the voice of an old nun who had taught us the skills of cooking in Drishane Convent many years ago: 'The secret of cooking is to turn a kitchen disaster into a dining-room triumph.'

How about turning a hare disaster into a deer triumph? Was that possible? Hidden along the bookshelves in the art room was a well-researched and beautifully illustrated book on the deer of Killarney that I had bought as a Christmas present for a sister a few years previously and had later fished back to enjoy myself. A long search ensued and the book was finally located – and into the rocking chair with me went a cluster of deer of all breeds and seasons, and we had a wonderful few hours together around the hills and lakes of Killarney. And as the book was absorbed and enjoyed, in my imagination the hare disappeared over the hill and a deer came across the mountains.

Back to the canvas, and slowly a transformation began to emerge. Over the evening hours my hare slowly but surely started to fade into oblivion and, very tentatively, an elegant mountain deer appeared. It was the most extraordinary and enjoyable trans-breed operation, if there is such a thing in the animal world. My annoying but honest art critics had helped to turn my disaster into a triumph. I might not have caught my hare, but the deer was looking good! Maybe someday I might catch the hare?

A Gaggle of Geese

Now that I am living on my own I really take the time to sit down and savour my post. What a pity it would be if the art of letter-writing were to die out. Isn't it great to get a long, newsy letter in which the writer takes you into their world? Isn't it great too when you open your post and out comes a 'Wow' card. Not only does the card give you an immediate spurt of initial delight but having savoured its contents you can then display it on an advantageous perch somewhere around the house from where it can send out rays of pleasure and positivity for days or even weeks, depending on your connection with and appreciation of the subject matter. Cards such as these are bright flowers along the path of ordinary life, but during lockdown, especially if you live alone, they can be the stepping stones to survival. One of my display points for these cards is the top of the television – and maybe I should explain that my television is confined to a press because the blank face of a TV, when not turned on, is not a cheery presence in any room. So, when not in use, mine disappears into lockdown in a press, behind two sliding doors.

For weeks in the early days of the pandemic, during what we then innocently termed 'cocooning' that turned into the

more realistic 'lockdown', a wonderful card with a photograph of gobbling geese sat on top of this press. I absolutely loved it. And every time my eye happened to fall on these birds, they brought a smile to my face. Geese and I have a long and deep-rooted relationship stretching back to the days when they waddled around our farm.

On the wall above them, the prime viewing point in this room, hangs a large, beautiful painting of geese by Susan Webb. It has hung there for years and in that time has radiated out hours of endless pleasure. This artist knows her geese and on many occasions her picture has brought me to a standstill of appreciation, bringing an amused, remembering smile to my face. You can almost hear the flap of their wings in the flowing water of the river and feel the swish of spray over them and hear their honk of appreciation and communication to each other. Reared on a farm where geese were forever parading around the yard and fields, my mind absorbed their many oddities and peculiarities, and this artist captured them unerringly. It is impossible to quantify the endless pleasure that can be derived from a picture with which you make a special connection. And it does not have to be an expensive painting either. The pictures on our walls vary hugely in value, but they all bring daily enrichment and may sometimes tell the stories of our lives.

Having spent a week on the TV press, my goose card graduated to the top of my desk and finally onto the kitchen window. These geese were gradually making their way in the direction of the art room and finally they made it there and perched themselves on top of the easel. Every morning when passing that door on my way downstairs, I looked in at them, unsure if it was for the sheer pleasure of just seeing them or whether it could be a 'getting to know and absorb them better' process. It is at times like this that you wish you were an artist like Susan Webb. But, as one of my best friends constantly tells me: 'We have to row with the oars we have.' But right now I was wondering were my oars up to capturing this gaggle of contrary, squawking geese on canvas. I continued to study Susan Webb's geese and looked up any books that had pictures of geese, and actually there were very few available because geese seem to have some-how gone out of fashion. Some years ago, I used to drive by a large green field near Macroom that was full of the most gorgeous fat geese. It was an enchanting never-to-be-forgotten sight. But now there seemed to be nowhere to study these contrary creatures.

These amazing birds peck their way into the world out of enormous white goose eggs hatched into life by a large, loving mother in a nest that can only be described as a work of art. Mother goose prepares her nest with the careful application to detail that an expectant human mother pre-pares the crib for a firstborn. She scoops out her nest in the middle of a large bundle of hay or straw and shreds the sops into soft wisps with her strong yellow beak, while darning through them tiny bits of downy feather eased off her own big, soft, white bosom. She goes around in circles darning all these natural materials together until she has woven a soft, circular, warm cradle of comfort. When she is happy that all is to her satisfaction, she settles herself in on top of her giant eggs and lovingly hatches them into life with the gander father on standby duty beside her. This father has strong, responsible paternal instincts and looks after his progeny with care and attention from beginning to end. After four weeks the baby goslings begin to crack the shells open and then soft little yellow bundles of delight begin to emerge and are cared for lovingly by both parents. As soon as they get their long spindly legs under them, these gorgeous goslings are led through the farm fields to the river, with the vigilant father keeping unwelcome nosey parkers at bay. Quite quickly they grow into strong, leggy teenagers and by summer are indistinguishable from their parents and have developed all the quirky, enchanting mannerisms of adult geese.

But the challenge for me now was to capture these magical mannerisms on canvas. In some ways, painting is a bit like writing because you may begin with one idea, but, as you progress, different ideas can sprout out. But it takes a bit of blind faith to take the first step. To jump in. To simply get going. And, hopefully, once started, the mental images of the geese on the home farm and their honking that I hear in the air around me would do the trick. Having them in my head and mind's eye was one thing, but getting them to land on the canvas was quite another story.

However, once the first spurt of paint hit the canvas, the die was cast and thereafter came hours and days of frustration,

self-doubt, 'stickatitness', delight and dedicated determination. During this time it is vital to walk away from the canvas and give oneself and the geese a break, otherwise, unlike mother goose and her nest, my canvas could end up in a pure puddle of muddy confusion instead of the intended peak of perfection. On returning later there could be a sudden breakthrough. That is the blind hope – that a remembered curve of a neck or the flash of a yellow beak can be achieved on canvas. You know instinctively when this breakthrough happens and it is these little bursts of 'getting there' that hang like golden apples along this sometimes tortuous path of paint.

This period of sometimes painful progress results in very early morning trips while still in night attire to the easel to judge, with the clear-headed perception of these early hours, the level of success or otherwise being achieved. This is the hour for honest appraisal which can be full of the ecstasy of success or the agony of failure. Is there skill, training and expertise involved here? Undoubtedly. But I have very little of these – and here I must apologise to Lia Walsh of Cork Art Supplies who gave us our first art classes when she was living in Innishannon, and to the saintly and gifted Brother Albert of the Cork Art Society who endeavoured, patiently, in his night classes to endow me with these abilities. But mastery of the complexities of the skills meant the discipline of adhering to a limited palette, which I found difficult. But despite all these shortcomings – no reflection on my mentors, but rather my own lack of discipline and artistic ability – the joy that trying to paint has brought me over the years is tremendous. And during cocooning and lockdown it has been one of my sanity savers. So, it was a case of 'keep on keeping on' and occasionally catching glimpses of the possible. The geese and myself wrestled it out together and eventually, as with the mother goose's nest, the project was complete. Maybe not as perfect as her achievement, but sufficient to satisfy my own not-so-high standard.

Because I was so happy with the result I decided to turn it into my Christmas card because to me geese are synonymous with Christmas. So I would inflict my card on my friends, who hopefully in the special season of goodwill would view it kindly. In conjunction with the Christmas cards, I also ordered blank cards for around-the-year use. Who knows, but one of these cards might cause someone somewhere to smile and say, 'Wow'?

History in Our Heads

By the time this pandemic will have said farewell to us, which will hopefully be sooner rather than later, we will all be Olympic fit, as waves of walkers have taken to the highways and byways of country roads, many trailing leads with dogs of all sizes and ages attached. Because this virus stripped away our normal social interaction, these walks have turned into our new communication channels. On these outings, social distancing poses no problem as 'across the road' conversations are the new norm, and the medical experts are advising that the great outdoors is the replacement for the fireside chat. Covid has thrown up many challenges but some of the minor day-to-day ones can, with time and planning, be circumvented. This circumventing may take a little longer, but is still doable. And so new chatting channels have opened up along the quiet roadways between neighbours who previously simply did not have a minute to bid each other the time of day. Also, messages and books are stealing in through letterboxes like thieves in the night. This virus, with all its crippling limitations, has surprisingly given some of us more time, especially those of us

living on our own without children to home school.

These open-air exchanges have thrown up a variety of topics, sometimes intriguing, depending on the familiarity and communication skills of the walkers. Topics could range from the weather to local affairs, to books being read and exchanged, to prevailing political conditions national and world-wide. The American presidential election and subsequent fall-out provided endless discussion, and the strange anomalies arising from Brexit — and, of course, Covid, always the Covid, and how we were all coping and surviving. Occasionally a surprise topic might jump out and bring you to a standstill, providing much food for thought on the ensuing journey.

This happened to me one Saturday as I walked through the churchyard on my way for a ramble along Bothar na Sop, which is a narrow, leafy little lane deriving its name from the fact that it was once lined with thatched houses. In the churchyard I was greeted by a man with the salutation, 'Now, you might be just the woman to tell me something that I am trying to find out.' 'Well, that depends on what you are trying to find out,' I told him. As I am a blow-in (though I have lived here sixty years) it always surprises me to be asked questions about Innishannon by a local. But maybe this is due to my interest in its history, so it's probably a case of 'where the heart lies there the treasure is.'

'Could you tell me,' this man asked, 'where Peacocke is buried?'

To say that I was taken aback by his question is putting it

mildly because Peacocke is a name from the past that I had not heard mentioned for years. And really I knew very little about him apart from the fact that he was one of the Anglo Irish landlords who had lived in one of the great houses in Innishannon, with a large tract of land attached. I had often read the name on a stone plaque at the entrance to the little Church of Ireland graveyard up the hill from where we were standing, and the inscription on that plaque conveyed the fact that the ground for that graveyard had been gifted to the parish by a man named Peacocke; the inscription was fading but presumably this was the same man. Peacocke, unlike Murphy, O'Sullivan or McCarthy, is not a name you come across every day in West Cork. While all this was running through my mind another startling revelation emerged: 'My father shot Peacocke'. If I was surprised by his first statement I was thunderstruck by his second, and looked at him in amazement, too mesmerised to ask any probing questions. 'I have no idea where Peacocke is buried,' I told him, 'but it should be easy enough to find that out.'

This extraordinary exchange gave me much food for thought on the rest of my walk along the Mass path beside the church down into Bothar na Sop, and on a short stretch of the busy main road, and then thankfully back along the much quieter Bothar Daoibhinn, 'the idle road', so called because it was created during the Great Famine to provide wages for the starving people whom the powers in charge judged had to work to earn an honest crust for their survival. All over the country these useless roads were created for such purposes, and now, even though much busier than in earlier days, many have become wonderful walks along which run hedgerows full of chirping birds and the sound of running water in deep dykes.

Arriving home I went on Google and to my surprise found an amazing amount of information on the said Captain Peacocke. He had lived with his widowed mother in a house known as Skevanish House, which came as a bit of a surprise as I had never heard of such a house in the townland of the same name, which is just beside the village. The report stated that on the night of Saturday, 31 May 1921 two members of the IRA (Irish Republican Army) went to his house and shot him. It stated that the following Saturday he had a large funeral and was buried in the 'new Protestant burial ground which was presented by the deceased to the [Protestant] parishioners of Innishannon in memory of his deceased father. All shops were closed and blinds drawn as a mark of respect for the memory of the deceased and the funeral was large and representative of the local gentry and the people of Innishannon.'

It came as a bit of a surprise to discover that he was just thirty-two years old – one somehow always assumes that retired military men are of the elderly variety. The IRA men involved were probably in their late teens or early twenties. This report went on to reveal that in the following days the house was burnt down and all the cattle taken off the land. It made for sober reading and brought back an Innishannon long, long before my time.

The following Sunday, a bright sunny day, I made my way up the hill to the little graveyard where I now knew Captain Peacocke to be buried. It was odd that whenever he was recalled locally he was always referred to as 'Captain', though his actual military title had no mention of Captain but the higher rank of Lieutenant-Colonel. But for some reason, in local minds the term Captain had remained attached to him.

Christ Church graveyard is east-facing so, like Cormac Mac Airt, all buried here face the rising sun. I had attended the burials of many neighbours here and would often call to say hello to these buried old friends when passing by. But on those occasions my visits were always to the more recent plots, so I had never actually gone around to read the inscriptions on the very old headstones. But today that was my mission as my quest was to locate Captain Peacocke's headstone, and he had been buried here 1921. By a strange coincidence, this Sunday was the centenary of Bloody Sunday in Croke Park in 1920 when people attending a match were shot by the Auxiliary British forces.

After opening the gate into Christ Church graveyard you need to climb a very steep ramp, along which you are aided by a rail attached to a supporting wall and on this wall is the plaque stating that the graveyard was donated to the parish by Lieutenant-Colonel Peacocke on the death of his father, who was obviously the first to be buried here.

So I walked slowly between the headstones, seeking out the oldest stones along the back and in the process came on the name Stennings, which rang a memory bell – another

IRA shooting at the time. For some reason his shooting had been much more talked about later in the village than Peacocke's. Was it because he lived in the village? He too was shot in his own home, which was also later burned, but pictures of that house in all its elegance are now part of the famous Lawrence Collection, which recorded many of these old stately homes before they were burnt. Stennings's house, which was known as Innishannon House, was later to become a garage and is now a supermarket. Only this headstone remains as testament to the man who had once owned a large part of the village and acted as agent for the Frewen family, who were the landlords.

Walking around the graveyard and reading these historic inscriptions was a strange experience, bringing alive Ireland's troubled past. Eventually, by process of elimination, I came to two weather-bleached headstones just in front of the entrance – two simple, solid, stone crosses from which time had totally obliterated the inscriptions. These, I concluded, could be the headstones of the two Peacockes, father and son, standing one behind the other. Needless to mention, after what had happened to the younger Peacocke, his mother had gone back to England never to return, and now all that remained of this family were these two headstones. It was a strange feeling standing looking down at these old weather-beaten headstones one hundred years after that tumultuous time. Was this the answer to the question that had led me on this quest? In the process many sleeping ghosts of the past had been awakened and

the realisation that some of our unrecorded history is still resting in the memory of those involved.

On the following night I watched an excellent RTÉ documentary on Bloody Sunday in Croke Park which now had much more relevance for me as a result of my own uprooting of our local turbulence. Our graveyards may be the final episode where both sides of our story are recorded.

the Remains

ho dep d th

aged Si y s

oorke June

And his D

Thoorke S

No i

Written in Stone

One hundred years ago in 1920-1921, Ireland was going through a traumatic period. Recently on TV there were programmes on Bloody Sunday, the Kilmichael Ambush and the Burning of Cork. My search for the Peacockes' grave, linking back to that time, created in me a new awareness of our tumultuous past.

Also in the little graveyard I had been exploring was the headstone of Mrs C, the lady from a similar background to the Peacockes who had shared our home for twelve years before she died. She too was from an Anglo Irish background and came from the West of Ireland where their home too had been burnt during those troubled times – she indignantly complained to me, 'We were far more entitled to be there than the people who burnt us out because we were one of the oldest tribes of Aran.' She was a stalwart lady from whom I learned a lot. When her end was in sight she informed me that she had left instructions with her legal representatives that when her limestone cross was erected beside that of her husband, who was already buried there, both graves were to be covered over with a limestone slab. She said, philosophically, 'In future years there will be nobody here to take care of our grave.' She was never slow to grasp the briar of life and now when visiting her grave I smile and remember her clear-sighted assessment of this future reality and recall how interesting she was in so many ways. Her funeral, in 1993, was, to put it mildly, a little tricky to coordinate due to her diverse lifestyle, but also because of the limited inter-Church integration of the time.

When she died she had one son at the other end of the world and another in the south of England, a charming man whom I had met on many occasions, and she also had a step-daughter in London. On the morning of her death I got a call from the son in England and the step-daughter, both charmingly informing me that as they knew absolutely nothing about arranging funerals, least of all an Irish funeral, they wished to leave everything in my 'capable and knowledgeable hands', and that they would arrive when all was arranged. The only specification was that one of my poems which she loved was be read at whatever format her departure would take. Mrs C had not shown the slightest interest in her future funeral arrangements, considering them to be of no consequence whatsoever. So I was left holding the baby, or in this case, the body. And now it was a question of endeavouring to do the right thing. But what *was* the right thing? Funeral arranging can be a bit tricky at the best of times, but when you are not a family member and the circumstances are slightly unorthodox it is more so.

She had been reared Catholic, but over the years had acquired three husbands at a time when divorce was not an acceptable option, so, as she informed me, 'When you break the rules you leave the club'. Were her policy to be widely embraced, I thought, most clubs would have very few members! However, despite leaving the club, she still had great respect for the Catholic ethos and had strong ties to her beliefs, and so I felt this needed to be acknowledged in her funeral arrangements. Her husband was buried in the Church of Ireland graveyard across the road from St Mary's Catholic church, so whatever took place in the Catholic department we needed to finish up across the road in the Church of Ireland one. After a lot of toing and froing, the plan that eventually evolved was to have Mass in the Catholic church at one side of the road followed by her burial in the Church of Ireland graveyard across the road. Luckily, both clergymen, though a bit bemused by the proceedings, were willing to facilitate whatever I came up with, though it was the Catholic priest who had the bigger involvement because once we got across the road we would be more or less home and dry. All was going according to plan with our very helpful priest, but he baulked at doing her eulogy as he asserted that he knew absolutely nothing about her, so he insisted that I do it. Then it was my turn to baulk as, at the time, it was unheard of for a lay person to do that. 'But that's against all the rules,' I protested. 'We've them all broken already anyway,' he told me.

So we sorted things out the best way we could and we all did what we felt was required of us in a ceremony that included a diverse selection of hymns favoured by all denominations and attended by an upstairs-downstairs congregation. All went according to plan in the church and she was then borne across the road and laid to rest beside her husband. It was the first time that a funeral would encompass both sides of this road, appropriately known as Church Hill. When I visit her now, as I often do, in her high sunny perch, I recall her valiant spirit and unusual send-off, with which I feel she would have been very pleased.

On searching for the Peacocke's burial place I called to see her and noticed that the two limestone crosses and her ground slab were weather-beaten and the lettering growing illegible. She would not have approved of this, at least not while I was still around. So, standing at her plot, a decision was reached that an overhaul was overdue and I needed to get the stones cleaned. Then my eye drifted over to the nearby sad-looking little abandoned crosses and the thought came into my mind: why not get the two of these cleaned as well? Then at least there would be a visible record of where this father and son were laid to rest. Herself beneath the slab would consider this to be a great idea and could well be inspiring it from on high!

So, working on the premiss of 'never suppress a good impulse', I emailed Jim who, many years previously, had erected the stone on our family plot that will eventually bear testament to the fact that I too existed and that this little plot is where a stop was finally put to my gallop.

But that night doubts begin to emerge. Had I the right Peacocke grave? Maybe that could be the wrong grave, and how sure was I that father and son were actually resting beneath those two little abandoned crosses? Could I finish up cleaning the wrong headstones? After all, I had only reached my conclusion by a process of elimination. I could very well have got it wrong, and that would be a serious blunder. Headstones are sensitive territory and having someone from up above proclaiming the wrong occupant down below, or even cleaning the wrong stone, does not bear thinking about. Could I unwittingly end up running up the steps of a High Court? Alarm bells were going off. It was best to make sure. But how? By what process could you ascertain who exactly was beneath a headstone when the inscription was no more? Church records are available though sometimes these may not be totally comprehensive, and researching them involves a lot of laborious work and time. And time was not on my side. I was working on impulse, which can sometimes land you in a whole heap of trouble. So I had to find another solution to the problem. But how? And then a memory box snapped open and out popped a solution.

About seven years previously, when, for historical reasons, it was decided to record the headstones in all the old graveyards around Ireland, I had been involved in rounding up our local team of volunteers, and amongst them was my friend Jerry, who also had a huge interest in our local history. I had watched him exercise his detection skills on an old headstone in a forgotten graveyard at the other end of the parish, and though amazed at the results which deciphered the lettering, I did not remember the exact details of the technique. So I rang Jerry to get an update on the process, and as he relayed his instructions he enquired, 'Would you like me to go up and do it?'

'That would be just great,' I told him, feeling sure that he would soon call back confirming my opinion.

But I was in for a big surprise. Half an hour later the phone rang. 'That is not the Peacocke grave,' Jerry announced.

'What?' I exclaimed in amazement. 'So who is in there?'

'On one stone is the name Campbell and on the other is Cook.'

'So where is he?'

'No idea, but definitely not there,' Jerry declared.

'Do you want to come up and have another search?' I asked.

'Might as well.'

So a few minutes later both of us, masked and well togged out, as it was a freezing cold day, were meandering around the uneven ground of the graveyard in search of a clue. Then Jerry called out, 'Come over here and have a look.'

He was standing in front of a large plot surrounded by a deep kerb and at the back stood a tall, impressive-looking limestone cross. But the only inscription on this cross was: 'Thy Will be Done.'

However, lying at the front of the cross was a separate plaque on which two names were inscribed, one being a long, double-barrel name ending with 'née Peacocke'. Could this be it? But this lady was born in 1923, two years after the two Peacockes had died and the mother had left

Innishannon. So how could this name on the stone be from the same family? Or was this pure coincidence?

On returning home I went on the computer and into 'HistoricGraveyards.com', but with no success. I could not even find Innishannon! Just then a son living in a faraway place rang and I immediately immersed him in my search for Peacocke. He went on his laptop and got instant success, which did not surprise me as he is a whizz at it compared to me. He announced triumphantly, 'Found it.'

'How?' I demanded.

'I'll send you on the link,' obviously an easier option than trying to educate his dopey mother!

The wonder of modern technology never ceases to amaze and impress me, and now on to my screen floated our little hilly graveyard where by now I was familiar with every humpy incline. And there on screen was the tall headstone in front of which I had just been standing.

'But how do we know that's the right one?' I demanded.

'Read the accompanying text,' he instructed.

And, sure enough, there it stated, in an inscription to the south side and another to the north, that father and son were both at rest there. I had not seen this as we had not searched the sides of the stone. So I rang Jerry again and told him, 'Found it!'

'You went up again?' he said in surprise.

'No, but going up now. Do you want to come?'

'Meet you above,' he said.

I did a print-out of the facts and headed up the hill again.

On arrival I ran my hand along the left and right side of the stone, but there were no inscription indents on either side. So I reread the print-out again, more carefully this time, and saw the word 'kerb' and also 'south' and 'north'. So I looked along the kerb on either side of the tall cross and there, sure enough, were inscriptions on both sides. But they were impossible to read. Jerry arrived and got to work with his paper and crayon, and miraculously onto the paper came the inscription. To the right was the name of the father who was the first person to be buried in this graveyard in 1920, and to the left the son, who was buried soon afterwards, in 1921. So the lady on the plaque to the front was of the same family, and later on, after further googling, I discovered that she was married to the person named above her on the plaque and that they had two children, who probably had children who were still alive. I was glad, in an unexplainable way, to have found out that somewhere in the world there might be a family – hopefully one day they might come back to visit their ancestral grave and have their family headstone cleaned. But for now my search was ended.

The following day I met Jim beside my old friend Mrs C's grave and he studied the inscription that she had put on both stones. As a man who has spent a lifetime erecting and inscribing headstones, he made a very interesting observation. 'These headstones, now, have all the relevant facts,' he said. 'You know, people put a lot of irrelevant details on headstones, like: "beloved" and "loving", and sure, at the end of the day, that applies to most us when we are gone, but more important than anything else on a headstone are facts and dates.' How right he was, as I had just discovered.

When Jim was gone, I walked around between the head-stones of this now so familiar little corner and suddenly a blackbird appeared on a branch above Mrs C's headstone singing his heart out. Listening in awe to this gorgeous recital, I wondered could this be herself proclaiming her appreciation!

Gardening...

There is no end to the delights of a garden.
Gone are the days when my roses were flattened by
footballs and my backyard choked by old
bangers being reconditioned.
Now it is truly my room outside, where unless there
is a gale-force wind playing havoc or Jack Frost is
on a visit, I dine out on my own but never alone.
Every meal tastes better under a tree where the
birds entertain you and each day around you the
garden turns a new page of delights.
A garden is also a shared pleasure as gardening
friends never tire of discussing its highs and lows.
And planning and planting constantly fills you
with the joys of anticipation.

A Little Bit of Heaven

Our Lady had moved. No, I hadn't lost it and we were not back in the era of the moving statues. I moved her – twice! Some time ago she had been brought forth from her long-standing position in the house where for many years she had stood, forgotten, on a high shelf in a corridor, and taken out to the garden for the May altar, where she was in a far better location with her back to the wall of the Old Methodist Hall that borders the top of my garden, facing the sunny south. But with time came a change of mind that maybe this was not quite the ideal location for her. I decided that she did not look happy there, and seemed a bit small and lost with St Joseph towering tall in front of her. He is a six-footer, while her statue is smaller. Maybe Joseph was not very happy with the situation either because when they were down here on earth with us, he, like the late Duke of Edinburgh, was always one step behind the Queen. So even for reasons of protocol, her location and situation had to reviewed. Moving Joseph was out of the question as over the years he had earned his right of residence in his location, and, besides, moving him would require machinery and male muscle, which were both scarce commodities these days – in lockdown you learned to live within your limitations.

So, there was a need to think about Our Lady's location again. I have often confessed to being a ditherer. Now, ditherers drive everyone else mad, but for ditherers a hovering decision is a bit like a pebble in the shoe that you need to keep shuffling around until it no longer bothers you. Some years back there was a detective series on TV in which Columbo was the slow-moving yet deadly perceptive Head of Investigations, and one of his repeat phrases, when all the pieces of the case in question did not quite fit together like a complete jigsaw was, 'Something bothers me, Ma'am.' Well, something about Our Lady's location bothered me.

So what was to be done? Another garden survey turned up no solution, so the decision was parked for later. And next day, while busy redeeming a lily from the clutches of a red spider, inspiration hit like a flash of lightning. Because right there in front of me was the perfect solution to my problem – a royal throne-in-waiting. And, to put the tin hat on it, the throne was right in the middle of Uncle Jacky's old gardening patch where he grew his cabbages and spuds beside his homemade henhouse. And Our Lady would love it because she was never into posh surroundings, even though we who came after her tend to think otherwise. This throne-in-waiting was the solid trunk of an old cherry tree that had given up the ghost years earlier, but left its foot firmly in the ground, and was now wearing a rich, luxurious coat of dark ivy. And this old cherry tree had the fantastic advantage of having twin trunks, with the shorter one to the front and the taller to the back. The top of the shorter front trunk would be a great platform for Our Lady, with solid back support provided by the taller trunk behind. Perfect!

So, shooting straight across the garden – though maybe a more accurate description is 'treading carefully' in case of stepping on a loose stone and finding myself face down amidst the pots and pebbles – I manoeuvred myself in the direction of Our Lady. I grasped her firmly to my bosom and we did a very, very slow waltz, really cautiously, back across the garden to her throne-in-waiting. There she got a fairly bumpy assumption up onto her pedestal, but was eventually firmly plonked on her elevated throne where she was as near to heaven as I could get her.

> The kiss of the sun for pardon
> The song of the birds for mirth
> You are nearer to God in a garden
> Than anywhere else on earth.

What more could she want? This was the ideal location for her because from her perch on high she had a bird's eye view down over Jacky's garden, and as you walked along the lower path you had a similar view of her, and she created a restful picture enshrined in the branches of her shady bower. Jacky would be delighted to have his old friend in the midst of his much-loved little bit of heaven.

A few days later, Ellie, aged seven, came to visit – now that this was permissible – and when I told her that Holy Mary was hiding in the garden she went in search of her. But when Ellie got to a fork in the path she turned right instead of left, heading off in the wrong direction.

But I let her off, waiting to see how long it would take her to discover her mistake. But instead of a mistake, Ellie made an unexpected discovery and came running back, announcing breathlessly, 'Nana! I didn't find Holy Mary, but I found God!'

Wow! Some of us spend a lifetime looking for him! While I was still absorbing this surprising information her three-year-old brother, Tim, ran in brandishing a pruner that he had discovered in the back porch. With some speedy diplomatic interventions this lethal weapon was retrieved from between his little fingers and he informed me, 'Nana, when I grow up I'm going to be a gardener.'

'That will be great, Tim,' I assured him.

'Nana,' he said, 'when you grow up what are you going to be?'

What indeed? Good question!

Fake or Real?

While I was sitting in the backyard having breakfast, a loud flapping sound came from the garden. Was it real or was I imagining it? In lockdown you do a regular update to check that you are holding it all together. After assuring myself that the imagination had not run riot, I walked up the yard into the garden and stood there for a few minutes trying to locate the source of the racket. Having ascertained that it was coming from the high wall of the Old Hall, I walked cautiously up the path towards it, not quite sure what to expect. But as I got nearer, the source of the sound could be seen through the branches of the trees – a non-stop black flurry of frantic action. I approached the commotion slowly and edged quite close. A demented blackbird was so intent on attacking his reflection in a mirror on the wall that he was totally unaware of anything else going on around him. I could hardly believe what I was seeing. It was mesmerising, because the onslaught of his attack was so ferocious. You could almost touch him, he was so completely absorbed in his warfare with the mirror and impervious to any other presence around him. Beginning at the bottom of the mirror, where there was a little shelf on which he could stand, he spent a few minutes on the attack there, and then he took off and flew up and down against it, bashing all the while against his reflection. It was a miracle that he had not injured himself in the process.

But how could I assure this demented blackbird that there was no invading enemy and that his battle was with himself? I shooed him away, much to his chagrin, and he flew up onto the branch of an overhanging tree from where his unperturbed female companion had been viewing all the commotion. She was completely unfazed by the crazy behaviour of her partner, whereas I was worried that he might do damage to himself. So I put a length of timber up to block his view, hoping that this might solve the problem.

But when I returned soon afterwards the timber was on the ground and he was back in action. His partner was still perched on high, disdainfully viewing all the goings-on and making no effort to soothe his ruffled feathers. What on earth was the matter with him? I had no idea, so I rang John, our local bird expert, and explained the dilemma.

'Oh, he thinks that his reflection is another male invading his territory and competing for his female's attention,' John informed me. So this was why the lady blackbird was looking so self-satisfied from her perch on high. She had two males competing for her favours and was obviously delighted with herself. 'What do I do now?' I asked. 'Nothing,' John told me. 'Just let it be and he will go away eventually.' Which he did.

And even though his attack was worrying in case he might hurt himself, his conviction about his reflection had put the final imprimatur of authenticity on my fake mirror-windows, which had been installed the previous year in preparation for our annual Gardens and Galleries festival, for which many of our local art galleries and gardens open to the public to fund-raise for the local Tidy Towns activities.

If your garden does not quite reach the lofty heights of Chelsea or Bloom, and you still presume to open it to the public as a fund-raiser, as I do, you may feel a certain need to introduce variations to your gardening theme to provide ongoing interest over the years for the visiting public, especially return visitors. A garden lover, but not a knowledgeable gardener, my little bit of heaven, which greatly enriches my life, bears little evidence of gardening expertise, but, despite its shortcomings, it has still been opened as a fund-raiser for the local church, the hospice, the installation of village historic plaques and more recently for our annual Gardens and Galleries.

So before the last Gardens and Galleries, I felt that my garden required a bit of added variety for the regular visitors. For a couple of years the same dedicated supporters had been meandering around this tangle of confusion I call a garden, so I needed to up my game and give things a bit of a lift to provide a ray of added interest. But what? That was the question.

Sometimes in life once you have a question in your mind the answer sooner or later pops out at you. And if you are in the right frame of mind it comes sooner rather than later. But first and foremost you need to have the question in your head, and there was a big question in my mine. And then the answer came suddenly in through a window!

The stone wall of an Old Hall is the northern boundary of my garden, which is an ideal shelter belt from the northern winds as well as providing a pleasant backdrop to the meander of paths and steps in front of it. This high stone wall of what was long ago a Methodist Preaching Hall is now partly clad with ivy and a miscellaneous collection of other climbers, as well as a climbing rose. Intermingled in this entanglement are numerous nesting boxes, many surplus to requirements as the birds prefer the network of climbers and the deep crevices, large and small, between the stones for their nests. You would have to love this old stone wall despite the fact that there is no doubt but that it is providing a high-rise apartment block for the multitude of slugs who nightly issue forth in battalions to lay siege to the garden. But in gardening you have to live and let live. It was this old wall, the first focus when you come through the garden gate, that held the answer to my current garden problem.

One day at Griffin's Garden Centre I came across the solution. It was hanging right up there in front of me on a long, blank wall. Now, Griffin's wall was not as interesting as my old wall, but interest was cleverly added to it by a series of mirror-windows. How smart is that? One of the reasons for visiting garden centres and other people's gardens is to get ideas. And this was a great idea well worth stealing. But these were no ordinary mirror-windows. They looked like something from an earlier age, before plastic and double glazing turned all windows into endless reproductions of themselves. These windows had character. Not handicapped by the necessity of having to keep out the cold or seamlessly blend in with the contours of a modern building, these windows had the historical 'princes-in-the-tower' factor about them. Designed in spooky gothic-castle fashion, they somehow had a Dracula's dungeon touch as well. They were fake stone, needless to mention, but good fake if there is such a thing. So good that you could almost believe that you were back in another era, the era of John Wesley and my old Methodist Hall. They stopped me in my tracks, almost convincing me on first sighting that they were the real deal. Into my head floated an image of them in another location, *my* location. I could just see them on the high wall of the Old Hall. They would look just great up there. A marriage made in heaven!

Enthusiasm for the idea flooded into my mind and so a long, dithering process ensued. The dithering was not about buying them, as there was no question about that, but about how many and what size. To add to the dilemma, they came in a three sizes – small, medium and large – but, thankfully, all in the same design so at least the design decision was sorted. But size was the big question. One big window would be inadequate, two still insufficient, and three would be one too many. How about the medium size? But, for some reason, the medium ones did not quite hit the spot, whereas the small ones were gorgeous, and evocative of the little country churches that you often see abandoned since we have decided that God is surplus to requirements. These little windows seemed to plead: 'Please take me, I'm just what you want.' Decisions! Decisions! Decisions! Not an ideal scenario for a ditherer like me, but luckily Eileen was with me, the ideal companion in these circumstances. After allotting a certain amount of dithering time, a conclusive decision was reached, and three windows came home with us: two big ones and one small. This selection would bring variety to the view. Perfect conclusion!

But on arriving home another problem reared its ugly head. Location! Location! Location! How best to space them out along the high stone wall of the Old Hall? Now, I might belatedly add that these mirror-windows were no lightweights as the stone-like frames were actually made of solid concrete. So there was no question of lifting them up and running along the wall trying them for size in different positions. And to add to the problem, a man with a ladder would be necessary to mount these windows at the right heights. So the only solution was anticipatory visualisation. All locations had to be confirmed before the man with the ladder could be called into action. On previous such occasions he had issued an ultimatum that prior to subsequent summons all location negotiations had to be completed. His job was to erect mirrors not to enter into prolonged discussions on positioning. Got the message!

So Eileen and I had much debate about the exact positioning on the wall and whether the small one should be in the middle or at the end of the row. Eventually Eileen went home and the rest of the afternoon for me was spent indulging in anticipatory visualisation from the garden gate. The garden gate is the entry point from which this big new impression needed to be created. In my mind's eye, the windows went back and forth until eventually I was in a tangle of confusion, more mixed-up than the climbers on the wall. But eventually the mental fog lifted and confusion cleared. Ditherers get there in the end! The small window would go up at the western end of the wall beside the little stone porch, through which, in an earlier age, the faithful had gained access to their church. This little window and that little porch were the perfect pairing. Then the two large windows were mentally allocated their proportionally spaced positions along the wall to the eastern end of the Old Hall. I got it sorted out in my head, so Eileen came back to rubber-stamp the arrangement, and, then before a change of mind and another round of self-inflicted mental torture ensued, the man with the ladder arrived and with no preliminary preamble whipped a hammer into action and up went the windows on the stone wall of the Old Hall. They were an immediate success, reflecting the branches of the trees in front of them, which actually gave the impression of another garden behind the wall. The mirrors and the wall were made for each other and were in perfect union. They looked so authentic they could almost fool me. Even the man with the ladder was impressed!

The following day, my friend Rose, who is a fellow gardener but far more knowledgeable than I am, called and

we had our customary meandering walkabout of inspection and discussion. Gardeners never tire of walking and talking around their own gardens and friends' gardens, and always find some new botanical marvel to discuss. But on this walkabout, I had an ulterior motive, as this was a test run for my windows. Would Rose notice them? They looked so much part of the old wall and they were not attention-seekers, but I felt sure that she could not but notice them as the wall of the Old Hall is a big statement in the garden. But would she be taken in by them? That was the question, and the big test of their authentic look. As we walked along I sensed a preoccupied air slowly encompass my companion, and a puzzled silence ensued. Then she came to an abrupt halt in front of the Old Hall.

'Were those windows always there?' she queried.

'Did you not notice them before?' I asked vaguely.

'No! And I never knew that there was another garden behind that wall either,' she continued, with a mystified air.

'Imagine you never noticed that before now!' I said evenly.

She stood viewing the Old Hall with a perplexed expression on her face and then, suddenly, it dawned on her what she was looking at, and she began to laugh. We both had a good laugh. My fake windows had nearly fooled her, so in my mind they had passed their first test with flying colours. If they could almost mislead Rose, who was very familiar with the garden, they should certainly convince visitors. They had passed their driving test, as far as I was concerned.

So the mirror windows were now part of the scene and this morning had got their final stamp of approval from the jealous blackbird.

The Scent of a Rose

In the centre of the kitchen table rising out of a pencil-slim silver vase was a dark rich red rose. Its inner depths magnetically drew the eye in its direction, encompassing and stimulating a sense of wellbeing. Enthralled by its awesome magnificence, I bowed in appreciation and its gorgeous scent wafted up my nose and slowly soaked into my soul. A wondrous moment! How could you thank a rose for such a glorious combination of benedictions?

This rose had just made my day! Up to this moment it had been an ordinary day. But the rose switched on an inner light and the day took on a golden glow. Are such miracles sometimes hiding in corners waiting to be sniffed out? The slim, elegant vase was part of this glorious awakening – a silver-wedding gift from a friend with an appreciative eye for the beauty of little things. It was the perfect receptacle for a single rose and over the years had lovingly displayed them to advantage.

And, miraculously, there was a second rose too! The pair had come with their legs sticking out through a paper bag. Maureen had picked them in the garden of our old friend, Brother Mitchel, who has now gone on to a heavenly flower garden. His beautiful roses keep his memory alive

for us who had loved both him and his garden. The companion rose stood in a tall, slim, clear-glass bottle in front of a mirror on an old sideboard. This simple glass bottle, like the silver vase, perfectly displayed the beauty of this rose. These roses needed no embellishment beyond themselves, and they were in separate rooms as each rose needed its own appreciation space. The second rose was as glorious as its companion and the reflecting mirror accentuated its wonder. The pair were a double whammy of delight! Brother Mitch, who had created heaven in his monastery garden, had, like St Thérèse, left behind a shower of celestial rose petals. What a wonderful legacy for us who were the beneficiaries.

And so, having got the incentive from Mitch's roses, I wandered out into the yard and garden, sniffing out other miracles in hiding. It was a meandering, restful day, with no great activity in mind, which was a balsam to the spirit, especially now with Covid-19 skulking around making us all feel a bit uneasy. During this pandemic, some days could be irksome, but then along came days like this glorious one. A gift from the gods, they poured into the mind like warm, lubricating oil onto grinding wheels. Calming days like these were a gift, enabling us to find our equilibrium and inner balance. Sometimes, however, we might not be open to receiving these gifts and they could pass by, and we would never even know what might have been ours. But today I had my hands outstretched, waiting. Maybe Covid had made me more appreciative and receptive.

It was mid-July and we were nervous of another anticipated Covid surge. It was probably the price we were paying
for opening the cocoons, lifting travel restrictions, opening
up some sport facilities and allowing the bigger food-serv-
ing pubs to trade. But we had to test the waters and now
the waters were beginning to waver around us, and so the
scheduled opening of the smaller pubs was on hold. It was
a nervous time and the government was 'damned if they
do and damned if they don't'. It was a balance between the
economy and the health of the nation. So, in many ways,
though cocooning was officially over, we were still only
half-way out the gap.

Maybe that was why I was so appreciative of my two
beautiful roses and why I had mellowed into the mood to
wander around the garden open to whatever tranquility
might come my way. Today was a day for roses and so, drifting from one rose bush to another, I went along sniffing
like a cocker spaniel until I found myself, like a homing
pigeon, in front of the one that I had christened the 'Lisdangan Rose' after my home place. This rose had been bought
solely for its scent. A few years ago, as I was drifting around
a local garden centre, it caught my nose and awakened my
memory buds. Is there any other sense as evocative as our
sense of smell? Like no other faculty it can swirl us down a
memory road and spring open locked gates. And when this
whiff of my mother's roses assailed my senses I was once
again back in the home garden with my nose buried deep
in a big, fluffy, pink bloom that filled the air around it with

its soft, musky essence. Isn't nature all about soothing our senses of sight, smell and sound? In a garden we look, we smell, and finally we listen, because a garden is full of sound, and when you sit quietly a garden rustles all around you. But of all these elements, it is probably the smell of a garden that is best remembered. And nothing encompasses the wonder of smell quite like a rose. In today's world we have flori-bundas, shrubs, patios, climbers, ramblers and probably many other rose strains, but back in my mother's time most ordi-nary gardens just had roses. My mother's old rose bushes were indefinable as they had a multiplicity of legs and grew somewhat in the format of the furze bushes out in the fields. They grew as high and as wide as they wished, and were so spread out all over the place that the birds chose them as nesting sites. They were a vision of pink rose radiance, but it was their aroma that was their crowning glory. They imbued the air around them with this breathtaking cloud of deep, indescribable, but unforgettable scent. So that day in the garden centre the scent of this rose whipped me back through the decades.

Sometimes in early winter when the arching branches of my mother's roses were over-reaching a nearby path along which the stabled horses were led for water, my father got a hedge clippers and gave my mother's rose bushes a short back-and-sides. But they held no malice for his denud-ing and were back again the following summer, bigger and better than ever. Back then, as well as now, there was prob-ably greenfly, black spot and the countless other hazards.

But, left to their own devices, they all seemed eventually to cancel each other out.

Today in my garden this Lisdangan Rose, which is not as hardy as my mother's variety, cannot seem to make up its mind whether it is a floribunda or a climber, so you have to be prepared for any change of direction it might decide to take. Also, it blooms in clusters rather than in long single stems, so detaching a flower in bloom is a tricky business as forthcoming baby buds are in close attachment to the mother. So you need to snip with caution or otherwise you may unwittingly bring away an attached baby rose and be guilty of botanical infanticide.

That day, a well-placed bloom was selected and cautiously snipped, avoiding the nearby buds, and when this mature bloom was all mine, a deep, prolonged, smelling session was indulged in. This bloom was voluptuous, soft and fluffy, requiring a little pot to do justice to its overflowing abundance. The hall was the location of choice for this pink lady, and there she glowed softly in its cool shadows. The scent of a rose is a great comfort when the waters around you are wavering.

Gatherings

Having family and friends within shouting distance is a great comfort and being part of your community is an enriching experience because in any voluntary group there is a diversity of people and opinions that keeps life interesting and your mind alive. During lockdown when we were cut off from all this human interaction, this was really brought home to us. We might annoy the living daylights out of each other and at times drive each other crazy, but we still need each other.

And God Made Sunday

I n recent times our Church has been brought to its knees – maybe not a bad place for a Church to be! The old authoritarian approach has been weeded out and, as all good gardeners know, an in-depth pruning cuts out the dead wood and encourages fresh growth. A whole new Church is gradually emerging, but, like all new growth, it is slow and tentative. And then, to present further challenges, along came Covid-19 and lockdown! But could it be that in coping with the challenges of this virus the Church would recover its original focus on healing, forgiveness and kindness?

A few weeks after emerging from complete cocooning I got the urge to walk up to the hill and see how things were looking around our own church. Seeing the locked doors for the first time was a shock to the system, because no matter what trauma, be it famine or war, that engulfed churches down through the centuries the doors always remained open. Old churches absorbed and weathered many storms, and in the process became quiet, sheltering retreats. In recent years their silent interiors were probably one of the last bastions of quiet solitude in a roller-coaster world dominated by noise and clamour. We were all on a fast-forward conveyor belt and if you opted off the conveyor belt it simply drove over you, but now the conveyor belt had crashed and we had all fallen off.

Our church here in Innishannon, like others around the country, has not just one door but three and seeing all of these three large, gothic-style doors firmly closed – and firmly bolted from the inside – was a strange sight. They had taken on the appearance of locked prison doors. One felt like protesting, '*Et tu, Brute?*' Or demanding, 'God, where are you when we need you?'

For the previous few Sundays Fr Finbarr had said Mass in an empty church, and many of us, even those with inadequate computer skills, endeavoured to stay connected via Facebook, a new and testing experience for all concerned. We were now also finding out that Mass attendance was about more than the religious service itself, but that the church was also a place to meet up and stay connected with friends and neighbours, and for newcomers to get to know each other and the locals. Fr Finbarr also had a strong link to the school, so the children too were always involved in church activities – bringing up the gifts at Mass, saying the Prayers of the Faithful and handing out the newsletters. This artery of community was now temporarily severed, leaving a big gap. Now too, the Covid-19 funerals, following the health-and-safety guidelines, were a much shrunken experience and instead of gathering in large crowds, friends and neighbours stood in a guard-of-honour along roadsides and streets to acknowledge the passing cortège and support the bereaved. Mourners reported finding this practice extremely comforting. How we will progress from here on remains to be seen. At the moment we are living in a constantly changing social landscape.

Fronting our church here in Innishannon is the usual ugly, though necessary, tarmac church carpark, but its grey face is thankfully redeemed by a rosary of beech trees encircling it like a collar. Also from around the back and along one side is a well-kept, meandering cemetery, where departed members of our parish rest and where inevitably many of us will eventually join them. But not yet! And hopefully not fast-forwarded there by Covid-19.

Old cemeteries such as ours are part of parish life and walking around here can be very restful and informative, so many people when visiting the church go for a walk-about. Weathered headstones are, in many ways, historical records and maybe there is a need when erecting new ones or adding fresh inscriptions to old ones to be specific in recording location details and dates. Anything cut in stone has a tendency to survive, and posterity and historians will thank us for any historical details we leave behind on headstones. It would be regrettable if, in replacing this system with cremation, we all finished up in little boxes on shelves in the walls of mausoleums. Maybe the solution would be to merge the two systems, with our ashes returning to our family plots to be recorded on the headstone beneath which entire clans could be laid to rest. The best of both worlds!

Ours is not the modern idea of what a well-laid out, orderly graveyard should be, but a collection of all kinds of interesting remembrances humping up and down with the lie of the land. It is maintained by a voluntary group who come weekly to do a tidy-up and the result is that it is a peaceful, restful retreat corner in which to ramble around and visit old friends.

Buried Free
When I die
Don't bury me
In a military-style
Well-kept cemetery
Where everyone
Lies in rows
Of well-organised
Parallel toes.
I'd rather be
On hilly ground
Where Mother Nature's
Abundance flowers;
Beneath a mark
Of natural stone
As bleached and grey
As will be my bones.
I could lie
Beneath a tree,

Whose whispering hair
Would shelter me.
Maybe long grass
And weeds would grow,
Better this
Than a disciplined row.

On my walkabout our own family plot was showing evidence of lockdown neglect and had turned into a mini jungle. My gardening soul overrode my free-spirit thinking, and so onto my knees I went to give it a quick overhaul. I ended up with earth-encrusted fingernails and unwelcome rose-thorn scratches! Should have gone with the free spirit!

Though the church was locked there were quite a few people drifting around and chatting across the headstones that were providing the necessary social distancing. On my walkabout I came across my friend Phil, and we perched ourselves on the kerbstone of two separate graves to catch up on mutual activities. We discussed the closed church doors and Mass online, and then Phil told me: 'I go to Mass in Boherbue some evenings at 7.30.' 'Boherbue!' I echoed in amazement as this was a little church on the Cork–Kerry border beside where I had gone to school and had been confirmed.

'Yes,' she enlightened me. 'If you go on to the website churchservices.tv you can scroll down through a variety of churches and find Boherbue, and the priest there, a Fr Keneally, says Rosary at 7.10 and Mass at 7.30 every evening.

There's something restful and comforting about the whole experience, and now I go fairly often.'

Apparently just before the first lockdown the Church had got a group of willing parishes on board to install the necessary equipment, and this brought their services online to be viewed by anyone who wanted to participate. A wise and well-timed step. It offered another kind of connectedness when we really needed it.

That evening I sat myself down in front of the laptop, full of curiosity, and carried out Phil's instructions. After a few false starts, I arrived into the church in Boherbue. To me the wonder of modern technology is still a bit mesmerising and I am always delighted and slightly amazed when I arrive where I planned to go.

Like many in Ireland I had grown up with the nightly rosary, but over the years the practice faded. Despite that, I found when death visited our home and all were traumatised, the rosary, in some unexplainable way, calmed the situation, even if some participants stumbled through the decades and needed some discreet prompting. Somehow the repetitive process became a calming mantra. I wondered about my reaction to an online rosary and to my surprise found it had the same calming effect. Maybe now that we were all subconsciously traumatised by Covid-19 we needed old, familiar comforters. Throughout the rosary, Fr Keneally interwove some lovely prayers of comfort from past Church heavyweights, like John Henry Newman and Teresa of Ávila.

May the Lord support us all the day long,
Till the shades lengthen and the evening comes,
and the busy world is hushed, and the fever of life is over,
and our work is done.
Then in his mercy may he give us a safe lodging,
and holy rest, and peace at the last.

John Henry Newman

And from St Teresa of Ávila, a visionary who built her convents near flowing water to sooth the spirit of her nuns: 'Let nothing disturb you, nothing frighten you, all things are passing, God never changes.'

The Mass that followed was equally soothing and enriching, and Fr Keneally called out the names of the townlands of the parishioners for whom the Masses of the week were being offered. For me it was lovely to hear the historic, poetic names of the familiar old townlands from around my childhood parish that I remembered since my school days. The names of our townlands, many in Gaelic, carry within them the deep roots of our history, and hidden in this culture and history are little forgotten treasures that await our visitation in times of need.

Then in mid-July the church doors reopened for limited numbers, and here in Innishannon, as probably in all other places, parishioners made the building ready. Sanitisers were installed, kneelers removed thus widening the spaces between seats, and each seat marked to accommodate three people in observation of the required social-distancing. Two

In the beginning

And the
WORD
was made
FLESH
and

dwelt
Among us
St. John
Chapter 1
Verse 14

IN MEMORY OF JER DESMOND
1916 — — 1999

masked parishioners stood at the door guaranteeing compliance with all regulations. We all arrived suitably muzzled and were directed to seats. People remained in their seats throughout, and Fr Finbarr himself did all the readings and then, donning a mask, brought communion down along the spacious aisles between the seats. Afterwards, people left slowly, observing the social-distancing markings on the floor. The whole ceremony ran with military precision. Outside the church, we waved or chatted to each other from a distance. Our sense of belonging to a community had survived. Over the next few weeks we adjusted to the new rhythm and instead of the usual large Sunday gatherings people spread out over four Masses throughout the week. It was good to be back.

Separate Tables

He arrived on the last day of 2019. A placid, happy baby, who beamed in delight at all around him and during his first few months was passed around like a happy parcel of smiling contentment. Then in early March came Covid-19 and we were all locked in and out, and he was held by no one but his parents for almost three months. We had entered a strange new world where we peered in and out at each other through windows. In early June a wider gap was tentatively opened and we hesitantly ventured forth and after a while I called to see him, but when his mother handed him over, this laughing baby cried in alarm. I had become a stranger! But he soon recovered his original happy friendliness.

His christening had been scheduled for early April and our cousin Fr Denis, who serves in Castleknock in Dublin and had married his parents and baptised his two siblings, Ellie and Tim, was to travel south to do the christening. The baby was to be called Conor Michael. Conor was in memory of our cousin and great friend Con, who was Fr Denis's brother, and had lived with us for many years and been so much part of all our lives; the name would also commemorate my little brother Connie, who had died aged four. And

Michael Gabriel was my husband Gabriel's full name, so Michael would be another loving remembrance. So, Conor Michael would be sheltering under three branches of his ancestral tree.

The April christening had to be postponed and when the churches reopened it was ascertained from Fr Finbarr, our local parish priest, that 22 July would be suitable for the rescheduled christening. Due to virus restrictions Fr Denis could not now travel south, and Sean, the prospective godfather, was living in a country not on the green list so could not fly home. Conor's christening would have to be a more curtailed affair than was originally planned, with numbers greatly reduced, so it was decided that to avoid bringing an extra person on board, which would add to the numbers, I would act as proxy godfather. The plus side to the postponement was that Conor was now a much bigger and more alert baby who could observe and enjoy the activities surrounding him. Given another few months, he would be able to walk to his own christening!

It was decided that an outdoor post-christening gathering in his family's garden was the safest option and would allow more family to attend. At the back of their house is a large sliding glass door, so if the weather behaved itself, the permitted number could safe-distance around this area. My son Mike had a small marquee roof which could extend their kitchen roof, but unfortunately one of the six long legs supporting this roof was in the need of a hip replacement and if conditions were windy, this roof might well do a *Mary Poppins* on us. However, the other five legs could be pinned down with heavy flowerpots that would hopefully keep them anchored.

Then, in the week prior to the christening, virus numbers began to rise and the county where some of Conor's family live went into lockdown. We were in a constantly changing landscape, and the virus was calling the shots. As the result of the rise in Covid cases, the number of people allowed to attend outdoor events slid down the scale, so two small tables would now easily accommodate the allowed number: the Innishannon family at one table, and the visiting family at the other. Not great for togetherness, but Covid dictates!

The weather on the day of the christening was also causing concern. My forecast-checking hit a very high frequency and first thing every morning Safari was consulted to see what the weather had in store. Nothing good! Just before the christening date Storm Ellen was heading in our direction with the south-west coast first on her hit list, and we were dead-on target. Scenes from *Mary Poppins* kept floating in front of my eyes!

But whatever about the weather, mother and baby had to be dressed for the occasion. Baby was all ready for his first big day, with a beautiful handmade lace and crochet christening outfit washed and waiting. And thereby hangs a tale. Before my firstborn arrived I bought a brand new christening outfit but I had neither the good taste nor the money to buy well, something that I later regretted and always planned to put right for posterity. So when we held an

'Innishannon Creates It' craft fair and a beautiful handmade christening outfit appeared, the time had come to correct my mistake. The fact that this beautiful outfit was made by a good neighbour added to its appeal. This wonderful woman subsequently washes it whenever the need arises, and she had now collected and washed it again for the April ceremony. Now, previous babies christened in it had been younger and much smaller than Conor Michael, who was now a solid bouncing bundle of jumping exuberance. A test-run was required to check for size, and our curious model was absolutely delighted to explore the floating ribbons of his lace bonnet and dress, which, thankfully, all stretched to contain his chubby contours. He was thrilled with his frilly boots and bonnet, which he promptly whipped off to test for taste. His mother's outfit, acquired for the April event, was on standby, so both mother and baby were suitably attired!

Needless to mention, Ellie, being a seven-year-old little girl, was next in line and full of enthusiasm about dressing up for this big occasion, but four-year-old Tim was not greatly interested in all the fuss and carry-on. However, when Ellie paraded around in her pretty new dress, I said to his mother, pointing at Tim, 'What about The Boy?' Then out of a bag came a little blue pants with braces, and a blue and white denim shirt with a blue bow. Suddenly full of curiosity, Tim donned this new gear and was very impressed with himself. He stood in front of me with a big grin on his face and demanded, 'Now, Nana, what do you think of The Boy?'

Then Ellie turned her attention to me, demanding, 'Nana,

what are you going to wear for Conor Michael's christening?' 'No idea,' I told her. 'Come upstairs now with me,' she instructed, 'and I'll pick out your dress.' So she led Tim and me upstairs where she rummaged through my wardrobe. She was not spoilt for choice as Covid had put a stop to traipsing around shops looking for new outfits, but eventually she pulled out a dress that was actually the best of what was on offer. But that was not enough for Ellie, as suitable shoes had to be selected too, and then she turned her attention to jewellery, which needless to mention filled her with delight.

The drawer of a dressing-table was whipped open and she peered with excitement at the contents, which unfortunately are more ornamental than valuable – but it was all the same Ellie. The more bling and the flashier the better, as far as she was concerned. She selected a traffic-stopping red pendant for me, then went to adorn herself. The more glitzy the better! Then Tim, thinking that he might be missing out on something, decided that he too should be part of this draping of chains and pendants, but finally went for an obsolete watch long past its ticking days. He slipped it on over his hand and had to push it up above his elbow before the expanding strap would stay put. All suitably attired, we trooped downstairs to parade in front of the cause of all the fuss, who clapped his hands in appreciation.

So, with all the outfits selected, we waited for Storm Ellen to blow in and hopefully be gone before the christening the following Saturday. She was due in on Wednesday night and with a bit of luck would have all her coattails gathered and gone by Friday night, giving us time to erect our wobbly extension roof.

Storm Ellen raged in, leaving nearby towns and villages flooded, with trees coming down all over the place, including a large tree next door to the christening garden to form a canopy over it. The danger could be dead branches floating down on top of us, but a neighbour who has a tool for all occasions came to the rescue and with an extendable saw cut down the branches, much to the delight of Ellie and Tim, who viewed the action with excitement from a distance. Then Ellie industriously gathered up the smaller sticks for the winter fire, as she told us. The storm had passed, but that day a political storm blew across the country when politicians and legal heavyweights, forgetting Covid guidelines, gathered for a golf dinner – and that particular storm brought down more than wobbly trees.

The following day the allowed number of us walked up the hill for the christening, all suitable masked like gangsters on a bank hold-up. It was a beautiful ceremony and Fr Finbarr, who that morning had had a confirmation ceremony and two other christenings, still made us feel that this was the big occasion of the day, and went into great detail explaining the significance of the different oils used in the ceremony, to which Ellie listened with wide-eyed wonder – and given half a chance would have taken over applying the various oils herself.

Baptism is a beautiful ceremony with the symbolism of

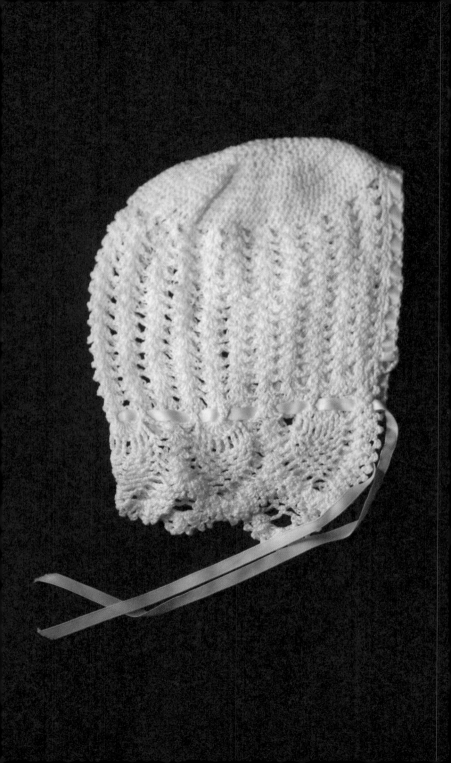

the christening candle being lit from the Paschal candle, and the christening shawl, signifying innocence, draped around the baby. Being proxy godfather and witnessing Conor Michael being christened with the names of beloved family members was a wonderful experience, and I prayed that his three namesakes would look over him and keep him safe, and that life would be kind to him. Maybe as we mature we become more appreciative of the richness, rituals and reverence of sacred ceremonies.

Afterwards we walked down the hill into the backyard where we carefully arranged ourselves in designated chairs around two tables under the long-legged roof that was still holding good. This wobbly roof gave the guarantee that should rain come suddenly, which looked very likely, we would not all have to run for cover carrying our food, all pre-plated to reduce any unnecessary intermingling. We were safely distanced, so conversation was carried on in raised voices. Not greatly conductive to togetherness, but all achievable.

Due to Covid-19 Conor Michael's christening day could not follow the usual format, but nevertheless would be remembered as a special occasion when twelve of us celebrated at a distance around separate tables. Such a different form of community, but a community nonetheless.

Sign of the Times

In recent years book launches were the springboards from which many new books went into circulation, but they were also sociable events at which old friends and neighbours gathered and the new book was signed and baptised with wine, tea and talk, and launched on its way to whatever fate awaited it. Pre-Covid this was the norm, but nothing was now normal, so thinking caps were being donned and we were all having to work things out again.

My first few books went forth without a launch and I assumed that this would be the case for my latest, *Books from the Attic*, published in autumn 2020. It would go forth unsigned and unheralded! I felt a bit regretful that this book would not have a launch or at least a signing opportunity, because the good thing about signings is that you get to meet readers and chat to them – and they give you lots of feedback, which is very valuable. With *Books from the Attic* this opportunity would not arise and I was very sorry about this because in many ways I felt that this book was extra special as it incorporated extracts that were so well known and loved from so many familiar old schoolbooks.

After my first few books were published by Brandon Books with no book launches, Brandon acquired a super

PR person in Linda Kenny, who decided that we should cop-on and have a launch. The book in question was *The Village* and because a photo of a sculpture of our local Billy the Blacksmith shoeing a classy-looking horse was on the cover, it was deemed that someone from the racing fraternity should do the launch. So Noel C. Duggan was drafted on board. Both Noel C and I had been born in view of Mushera Mountain, which made that book launch a real North Cork event, even though the subject matter of the book was all about Innishannon on the road to West Cork. The launch venue was the great Con Collins Bookshop in Cork.

It was a wonderful night and was about far more than the launching of a book. It was a family gathering, a coming together of neighbours and friends, and altogether a heart-warming community occasion. It made me realise that a launch was a very good idea, but also caused me think that instead of bringing the people from West Cork and North Cork into the city centre, why not have the launch at home in Innishannon, which would be far more convenient for all concerned?

So the following launch, and many after that, were hosted at home in Innishannon. At that time we had a wonderful art gallery in the village, which had previously been a small shop and old cow house, and had been beautifully converted into an atmospheric space for displaying wonderful paintings. It was the ideal location for a book launch. Steve MacDonagh of Brandon Books and I decided that any future launch would be held in Innishannon.

But time brings changes and with the untimely death of Steve, Brandon Books, as I knew it, ceased to be and was subsequently taken over by O'Brien Press, a Dublin publishing house. When a another book came about, I assumed that the launch would be in Innishannon, but O'Brien Press felt that Innishannon was a step too far into remote rural terrain and requested that the launch pad be Cork City Library. Because at the time O'Brien Press and I did not know each other very well, I did not insist (I was minding my manners!) and we finished up in the Cork City Library, which was a splendid venue. But that night as I looked around at all the neighbours and friends who had had to drive in from West Cork and down from North Cork to the city centre for this launch, I was determined that any future launch would be at home in Innishannon.

Maybe the time had come for the Dubliners to taste country ways and discover that village living has a lot going for it? So the following launch was held in Innishannon and there was a dramatic conversion at O'Brien Press to village launches, and to my delight subsequent launches were all held in Innishannon.

But this year, with the pandemic in charge, there would definitely be no launch, so poor *Books from the Attic* would go forth unheralded and unsigned. But people were constantly coming up with fresh methods to overcome the limitations that the pandemic was imposing.

So when I got a phone call from Ivan O'Brien regarding

the forthcoming publication of *Books from the Attic* I wondered if he had some alternative idea in mind. And he had. After the usual pleasantries, Ivan got down to business and in his precise, articulate way, laid out his plan. It was then mid-August and the book had gone to print in late July. His plan was that the printers would dispatch the relevant page of a number of books to be signed, and I would return them when signed, and the printers would then bind up the book with the signed pages included. This process would eliminate a lot of in-between handling by many people which would be highly undesirable with the contagious pandemic limiting our lives. Sounded like a good idea! One would have to be impressed. The number of books for advance signing would be one thousand, and I had no idea how many surrounding pages would have to accompany the signature page and I forgot to ask Ivan, but one email did mention the word 'palette' which immediately painted a mental image of bulk. One thousand books means quite a lot of signing, but on the launch of my first book, *To School through the Fields*, I had actually signed 750 copies at the first book-signing in Eason's of Cork. But that was thirty-two years ago and a lot of water had gone under the bridge since then!

So, with raised curiosity, I awaited the arrival of the consignment and wondered about the size and weight of the forthcoming delivery. As I was a little apprehensive of the prospect of lifting and opening a lot of boxes and getting the book pages sorted for signing, I had provisionally lined up my grandnephew, Dan, to come to my assistance if necessary.

Previously, when pre-signed books were required for book shops, two O'Brien staff members had brought them, and they did all the lifting and shifting, and coordinated the procedure into streamlined efficiency. Now with Covid, all this handling and proximity was no longer desirable. So Dan and I would work out our own system once we saw what arrived.

Then, on the first Tuesday in September, a two-and-a-half-stone box, chockablock with book pages landed on my kitchen table. One thousand of them! On inspection, they turned out to be A3 sheets of quality glossy paper, white on one side and a soft apricot on the other, to be signed on the coloured side at the bottom right-hand corner. The plan was to have them signed and ready for courier collection by the following Monday. All this I could handle on my own so Dan was off the hook.

Now this could an onerous, boring project if one let it be, but by not thinking too much about it and signing whenever the humour was on me, I could take it in my stride. My plan was to have no plan! And certainly not to do long, tedious signing sessions, but to take a wad of pages out of the box, not too many at any given time, and sign until enough was enough. Then I put the signed pages into a separate box and did not return to signing until the spirit moved. It worked a dream. With no target deadline, it was simply a case of 'head down, arse to the wind and keep going' – the sound advice given to us as children by a local man when we faced the tough, boring job of picking spuds, beginning at the bottom of a long, long field.

The KINCORA
Raiders

PREPARATO

The interesting thing about signing in a bookshop is the people. With no people around, you needed to get into a free-flowing mood of being observant enough to keep focused on writing your name but detached enough to float along mindlessly. Sometimes I tried to visualise the person who would eventually handle the book and hopefully enjoy it. One morning baby Conor paid me a visit, and for a few hours as he happily rolled around the floor where I kept half an eye on him, the signing flowed effortlessly and the pages in one box reduced and in the other increased faster than previously. He had an inexplicable positive effect on the whole process – a psychologist could probably explain that one!

By Friday night all the pages were signed, stacked back into the original box, ready for courier collection on Monday morning. Job done! Or so I thought.

Do you believe in Murphy's law? In case you are not aware of it, Murphy believed that 'if something can go wrong, it will go wrong and at the worst possible time.' I did not agree with Murphy. But a few weeks after the box of signed pages had gone back to Dublin a call came from Ivan to tell me that some of the signed copies had found their way into the wrong shops leaving others who had requested them short. So, to correct this mishap, a man with a van would leave Dublin for Innishannon early the following morning to return as soon as possible with 350 signed books. So, maybe, after all, Murphy has a point.

Going the Distance

I t was Hospice Coffee Morning and normally my front room would be full of people drinking tea, coffee and sharing scones, cake and apple tarts that many of them would have brought with them. This is our usual system of fund-raising, where one person hosts, others bake and more help out on the day. It is a combined effort of friends and neighbours and so the Hospice Coffee Morning, as well as being a great fund-raiser for the hospice, is always a coming together of friends and neighbours.

But this morning, instead of the usual gathering, I was here alone with a notice on the front door asking people to put their donation in through the letterbox, and contributions were already coming through, which was great because fund-raising had been hugely affected by Covid-19, though people were making great efforts to circumvent this. On the table in front of me was a plate with an inscription which was the basis of this method of fund-raising: the 'Giving Plate' came to us the previous year full of beautiful scones, and was originally designed and created by an imaginative young teacher and her pupils in a small rural school to assist their fund-raising efforts.

However, one of the health guidelines issued to us at this

time of the year was a request to each one of us to halve our social contacts. For many of us already on minimum circulation, this meant: stay at home and go nowhere, which is exactly what many of us were doing anyway. We were, no doubt, doing it to protect ourselves, but also for the common good as we looked around and saw our health service doing mammoth work and the government, no matter what our politics, doing the best that they could.

We were over six months into the pandemic. On that decisive Thursday in March when Leo Varadkar sent his message from America announcing the first lockdown, we withdrew into isolation, probably thinking that this might just be for six weeks, and then all would be well. A sense of togetherness arose and with it a feeling of 'We are all in this together.' And it was probably better that we all thought like this. Because one thing that the pandemic had taught us was that it was very important not to allow the magnitude of the situation to overcome us and cripple our ability to cope.

Each retreat behind closed doors made us dig deeper to mine our coping strategies. Not a welcome scenario, but there was no choice! To use a time-worn phrase, we were between a rock and a hard place – the pandemic and the economy. There were no ready answers and probably in the midst of all this pandemonium the biggest challenge was to nourish and preserve our sense of survival and well-being, to hold onto that little flame of hope and self-belief that leads us on when things are tough.

But in many ways we felt blessed in that we had no corrupt

dictator, no war, no famine, and when we looked at those in charge in other jurisdictions it made us appreciate that we did, at least, have a responsible government. Not perfect by any means, but even if God were Taoiseach at this time he too would soon be perceived as a fallen angel. There are moments when I think of asking a friend of mine who does calligraphy to write out a poem to send to Taoiseach Micheál Martin; the poem would be Rudyard Kipling's:

> If you can keep your head when all about you
> Are losing theirs and blaming it on you …

With the numbers contracting the virus rising and falling, then rising again, and with some badly affected counties going in and out of lockdown to the annoyance of some and the approval of others, we were all being tested to the limit. People were growing battle weary, and the financial cost was fraying nerves. Church services had gone back online but churches remained open and people were slipping in to say a prayer and light a candle. Every time you called, the candelabra was glowing with lighted candles, so many people were obviously finding solace in this.

At home I lit a lavender candle which filled the air with a calming glow and restful essence. These candles are handmade by a company called Moth to the Flame in Kilkenny, where Larry, a most talented craftsman, was still working away behind closed doors, despite the pandemic. As we listened to the six o'clock news every evening, hoping for

a slide downwards, we mostly had to deal with a sense of apprehension as they climbed upwards. The health of people was the first priority, with the economy close on its heels, but it was a ferocious balancing act because if we erred too much on one side the other suffered. One would need the wisdom of Solomon to get all this right. Our social fabric had been carved away by the virus and even though we might annoy the hell out of each other and at times drive each other crazy, we still need each other. Through the year it felt as if we were walking on thin ice, hoping that it would hold and that slowly we would get there. And on this scary journey the one light that helped keep us all going was the goodness and kindness of each other.

Kindness
The goodness of your kindness
Kept me in my mind
Its worth could not be measured
It had goodness undefined
You held out a caring hand
When I was full of pain
Your thawed my frozen being
And made me live again.

Challenges in Isolation...

I have always been intrigued by people who choose the silent, monastic way of life, and often wondered how the nuns and monks stick with it for a lifetime.
And I did find that the isolation of lockdown certainly lent itself to meditation, and undoubtedly there is a great inner peace to be found during long periods of silence. However, I eventually came to the conclusion that it was probably not for me as I am a sociable animal by nature — and also because if things go wrong in isolation you are in big trouble!

Grounded!

In March 2020 we elderly butterflies were instructed by the government to 'cocoon'. Not a delightful prospect as many of us were accustomed to flying high, but we followed instructions and flew back to base, where we folded our wings and remained grounded awaiting permission to take off again. This was an extraordinary experience, which I wrote about in my book *A Cocoon with a View*. Then it was finally over.

The long-awaited coming-out day for us cocooners dawned grey, misty and overcast – this would put a bit of a stop to our gallop! Maybe the powers that be had had a whisper in the ear of God asking him to intervene and discourage a flood of us geriatric debutantes out onto the highways and byways. But for some unaccountable reason, not even clear to myself, I was in no particular hurry out anyway. Was it simply that I had got used to being inside? Whatever it was, on the morning of Tuesday, 5 May, on looking out at prevailing weather conditions, I decided that there were better things to be done inside rather than donning a raincoat, bearing a brolly and issuing forth into the mist. The second day passed, and still no urge to emerge.

Could it be that all these years, buried deep inside in me,

was a sleeping hermit who really liked this retreat from the outside world and did not want to go back to it? Was this something I should worry about? The enclosed orders and the monks on Skellig Michael have always held a special fascination for me. Was cocooning a tiny sampling of what their life was like? Was I actually liking it? Needless to mention, I was totally fooling myself as, in comparison to them, I was sitting in the lap of luxury. Could there be a much bleaker explanation for my reluctance? Had I become institutionalised? But this cocooning only lasted two months – could it happen that fast? Then I remembered the philosophy of an old neighbour of ours who, if we were busy planning a special day out, would decisively declare, 'We'll wait now and see how my body will be on the day. If the body feels like it, we will move.' Maybe my reluctance was simply a natural slowing-down, accepting process when perhaps the body and mind become more integrated? This was a comforting thought.

So it was not until the third day after the lifting of restrictions that this particular body felt like moving. And this inclination did not come until quite late in the day, almost as if my emergence needed to take place in the quietness and tranquility of the evening. I have always liked this time of day because by then the pace has slowed and the world is breathing more easily. By then we rushing humans have eased our constant fast-forward pace.

So I gently turned the key in the door and for the first time in fifty-six days I stepped out onto the street. To say that I felt fragile is putting it mildly – a bit like a chicken not yet ready to emerge from the egg or an apple not yet ready to plop off the tree. I had a slightly unreal and uneasy feeling, like treading on water but not sure if the water would hold firm beneath me.

'Outside' felt like a strange place. Strange and yet wonderful. Looking around, I was slightly overawed by the miracle of being outside again. And yet ... and yet ... I felt a hesitancy not to venture too far in case it might all prove too much for me. To be honest, I was a bit intrigued by my reaction to being outside. Into my mind came the question of how people who have been in jail for a long time cope with coming out. During cocooning I had read *The Sun Does Shine*, the amazing true story about a black man wrongly convicted of a crime he did not commit, but because the odds were stacked against him had spent thirty years on Death Row. His story came back to me now as I walked up the hill on my first outing after cocooning. I knew I was in the halfpenny place by comparison, but I was thinking that were I to reread that book I would be even more impressed by this extraordinary human being.

The hill was deserted. Not a person in sight. I breathed a sigh of relief. But why did I not want to meet anyone, I asked myself? That was not like me at all. Was it that I didn't know how to comfortably handle the two-metre distancing regulation? If someone else didn't comply, what would I do? I had seen through my window during incarceration that while most people followed instructions there were some who seemed to think the rules were for other people and not for them. How would I handle it if I met one of those people?

Half-way up the hill I walked into the little recess beside my daughter's house to check on her summer window boxes that had been over-wintering there. Hearing the footsteps on the gravel outside, my son-in-law opened the window to chat. Little Tim, aged four, on hearing the conversation, mounted a chair to see who was outside. When he saw me, whom he had only peered in at for weeks from the street outside my firmly closed window, a look of stunned disbelief flooded his face and he whispered in a shocked voice, 'Nana, who left you out?'

Storm in a Teacup

We were into the dying days of August and autumn was breathing into the garden. It was lovely now to sit out there late in the evenings watching twilight creep in and hearing the birds settle down for the night. The blackbird was the last to retire, but as dusk descended he too finally decided to call it a day and after his last chirp silence descended.

But while silence was seeping into the garden a chill was stealthily seeping into my bones. When I rose from my chair to go inside every joint groaned in protest. Realisation hit hard that it had got very, very cold and that my frozen joints were locked into rigidity. With this sudden awakening to my chilled condition, reality dawned that this might not have been my smartest hour, especially in the present circumstances with the Coronavirus flooding the country. I should have donned an extra layer before sitting out in the garden this late! The last thing I needed now was a cold or 'flu!

But that is exactly what I got: stiff joints, a runny nose, sore throat and a cough. Common sense told me that I had caught a chill out in the garden, but in a pandemic common sense goes out the door, so I was flooded with panic and

guilt. How could I have been so bloody stupid? What the hell was I thinking about?

And how could I be sure that it was only a chill? Maybe I *had* caught the virus? My stress levels shot up and I became a bundle of fear and guilt. If it was the virus, how could I keep everyone around me safe? To be sure ... to be sure ... I announced to all that I was going back into total self-isolation. I locked the doors again and told everybody to keep away from me. The medical experts on radio and TV were advising that the safest thing to do when in doubt was to act as if you had the virus. And of course I had the virus! My sense of the rational had gone up in smoke. Panic had crashed in. And the blame game was on, but there was no one to blame but myself. It is very difficult to forgive yourself for you own stupidity. When you score an own goal you are your own judge and jury, with Captain Paranoid as the head prosecutor. Any mitigating element is not allowed to be a factor in your own trial. Pure stupidity was now the final verdict.

Back into complete cocooning with me, but this time I had two new stable companions – fear and guilt. Not good sleeping partners. They blocked sleep at night and woke me up early in the morning. But remembering the words of my wise mother, 'A rested body heals itself', I did very little physical work and concentrated instead on meditation and relaxation exercises. It was a rough time but slowly the effects of the chill subsided and gradually the realisation dawned that my hour had not yet come.

Then came an unexpected gift, which eased my tension and kept me sane. This reprieve came out of the blue. One night in an effort to distract myself out of my own hypochondria, I went channel-hopping on TV and fell upon 'The Proms' on BBC Four. Now, I love the Proms! I have no knowledge whatsoever about classical music – but, I reckon, to enjoy a beautiful painting you do not have to be an artist and to love wonderful scenery you do not have to be God. For me the Proms are a case of letting the music pour over me and letting my mind float away with it. An audible and visual feast. Just what the doctor ordered. Listening to the music and watching the absorbed faces of the musicians as they poured their amazing skills into their magnificent instruments was an experience of rapture. The conductor too was mesmerising. A tall, impressive figure in a black frock-coat, with a mane of white hair, he appeared to become airborne, picking up the notes of each musician and with his baton blending them in the air with invisible threads with a look of total absorption on his face. It was food for the soul, and on that night my soul needed it so badly!

When the concert concluded I turned off the TV because after this experience any other viewing would simply be mind pollution. I remained sitting in the darkened room, gazing out across the quiet street where the navy blue sky over Dromkeen Wood was star-studded around a glorious full moon. I had just witnessed the height of human achievement and now outside my window was the height of divine creation, and after one beautiful hour the traumatising effects of Covid-19 were gone.

The following morning my sister rang. 'Are you dead yet?'

'I think we could be at the beginning of a miraculous cure,' I told her.

'You just got your knickers in a knot about nothing,' she informed me. 'Common sense should have told you that you got a cold out in the garden. And you should have more cop-on than to be sitting out there at that hour.'

'Do you ever think you might have Covid?' I inquired curiously.

'Three times a day,' she told me, and added, 'the most important part of the body at the moment is the zone between your two ears. Holding the head and keeping calm is a big challenge now.'

'You are probably right,' I agreed.

A few days later the effects of my chilling experience had totally evaporated and gratitude flooded in. But I was learning valuable lessons and discovering that the fear of Covid carried with it a huge sense of responsibility towards the people around me. As a result I was now on a greater high-alert to the importance of hand-washing, social distancing and mask-wearing. Then I got another bit of advice from a son who arrived with an array of face masks that he had bought from a wise woman who had set up a mask-making business. 'Never be without one of these,' he instructed. 'In the present climate you need to have as many face masks as you have knickers.'

As Michelangelo declared in his later years, 'I am still learning!'

Not Now!

Have you heard of Murphy's Law? Well, Murphy declares that if something bad can happen, it *will* happen and at the worst possible time. Isn't Murphy a little ray of sunshine? He is the last fellow you would want to pay you a visit when you are in lockdown. We all have a Murphy in our lives and his female equivalent is a 'Wet Day Woman', whose aim is to spread doom and gloom. When you meet either of them you feel less well afterwards.

> All her thoughts were wet ones
> And all her thoughts were sad
> And anytime you met her
> You would regret you had.
> She'll depress you drip by drip
> And leaving you feeling low
> She is a wet day woman
> And will be always so.

But of the two, Murphy is probably the bigger pain in the butt because his theory, based on the law of averages, will inevitably sometimes be right. And recently in the pandemic he *was* right.

FLUSHED
WITH
PRIDE
The story of
THOMAS
CRAPPER
Wallace Reyburn

WASHING SO
500

The last eventuality you need in isolation is a breakdown of essential services such as power, water and sewage. But probably of the three, the most basic is sewage. This is a service that we all take totally for granted though the world owes a huge debt of gratitude to that unsung hero of the flush toilet, Thomas Crapper. Other inventors are much lauded, but poor Mr Crapper is recalled only when an abbreviation of his name is used to denigrate. I only became aware of Mr Crapper's contribution to our sanitary welfare when doing a book signing in a London bookshop many years ago where a very correct gentleman congratulated me on handling 'a sensitive subject quite delicately', referring to a chapter in my book *To School through the Fields* headed 'The Royal Wee' in which I endeavoured to describe the sanitary conditions of country living many years ago. This lovely man then presented me with a beautiful little book called *Flushed with Pride*, all about the life and times of Mr Crapper. But when Mr Crapper's invention fails to 'flush with pride' it causes great annoyance even in normal circumstances, but if you live alone, especially if you're in enforced isolation, which is a very fragile situation, it is a major crisis.

Now, if you're locked down in a rambling old house where all the facilities are antiquated, Mr Crapper's system is much more likely to collapse and Murphy's odds are vastly increased. And if there is one facility that could be described as fragile and antiquated in this house it is the sewage system. Installed well over half a century ago by an imaginative plumber, the teller of tall tales with a golden singing voice

– neither, unfortunately, contributing to expert plumbing skills – the sewage system has ever since operated on a bit of a wing and a prayer. As a result of this unfortunate situation, over the years my plumbing skills have been honed to the heights of meeting almost all running requirements as they arise.

A few years ago the constant repetition of this problem caused all the pipes in the backyard to be replaced. All but one little bit of piping, which, at the time, was difficult to access and thereby hangs a tale; as one Irish politician once famously proclaimed, 'It's the little things that trip you up.' And so it was that early one morning this little bit of sewage piping decided to act up. Unfortunately, the previous day had been particularly testing and my toleration level was at an all-time low, so I decided that a 'rest me' day was required to regain my equilibrium because isolation was challenging my survival skills. So, after resurrecting an exhausted body from the bed and indulging myself in a shower, and a body-and-mind overhaul, I eventually made it to the kitchen. So far so good. Hopefully this day would be better than the day before. Plonking the kettle on the Aga, and feeling that a bit of TLC was required, I put my breakfast on a tray intending to take it out into the garden to soothe my battered self. But before the kettle had time to work up a steam, a head appeared around the kitchen door. It was my son, Mike, who lives next door and had been keeping an eye on things at my house. He is always factual and to the point. He announced, 'The jacks at the corner is banjaxed.' 'Jesus,

Mary and holy St Joseph,' I wailed, feeling that I needed all three of these heavenly bodies to come to my aid. Ignoring his mother's over-reaction, Mike instructed, 'You go inside and I'll go outside. You know the drill.' I did indeed! Prior to the pipe renewal a few years earlier, this had been a regular rescue operation, which was dreaded and hated with a vengeance. But the one thing that you learn from experience are coping skills, and so, putting the kettle aside I headed for the problem toilet. The bowl was full to the brim, but fortunately only with clear water. In certain circumstances you have to be thankful for small mercies. The hand-basin had a similar problem. Boys, oh boys! Murphy was in full flight. Mr Crapper, where are you?

Then I remembered that buried somewhere in the bowels of the back porch or the garden shed – or at least that is where I hoped it was – was an enormous plunger. But a frantic search of the back porch proved fruitless and so I headed for the garden shed, circumventing Mike in the backyard where he was on his knees peering balefully down a gaping manhole. Thankfully, the giant plunger was swinging off the ceiling of the shed, with a host of other abandoned clutter. I grasped it like a drowning man a life-buoy. A few months earlier I had caught sight of this particular giant in an old hardware shop and, bearing in mind our dodgy plumbing scenario, had thought: You might come in handy someday. That day had now arrived. On my return through the back porch I donned a large pair of rubber gloves and an all-encompassing garden apron, having learned from previous experience that you needed to be robed up like a surgeon for the job on hand. I flung another pair of gloves out the window to Mike, who was in the process of forcing a gushing black water-hose down the yawning mouth of another manhole. Inside, I angled my giant plunger down the flooded mouth of the toilet, but its rigid swan-neck throat muscles resisted circumvention. Still, I persisted, in desperation thrusting the plunger up and down, but to no avail so I decided, like Fagan, that there was need to 'think this one out again'. Next a gigantic bath-towel was brought into action, as this at least could curve around the bend, but, after several desperate plunging and withdrawing efforts, this process was also abandoned. Under the kitchen sink was a bag of washing soda and this was the next effort towards a breakthrough. But still no shift. In the meantime, Mike was outside thrusting the long hosepipe in and out of the manholes. But the pipes were holding rock-solid. Like Brexit, not open to negotiations!

Then I got a brainwave and rang Martina in the shop next door to enquire about the availability of something stronger, and she suggested Mr Muscle, which she promptly dropped outside my front door. A lot to be said for village living! I ran an eye over Mr Muscle's instructions, which warned against mixing with other substances. But by now it was too late to be careful so I threw caution and a full container of Mr Muscle down the toilet bowl, hoping desperately that the collision with the washing-soda crystals would not create an underground earthquake. But not a sound came forth and unfortunately neither did a move. Mike was pursuing progress from the other end and we shouted our progress – or lack of it – in and out the toilet window.

I brought the giant plunger back into action, but after a few minutes of hard plunging the plunger lost its head, and I was left holding just the handle. I retrieved the lost head from the toilet and the giant towels came back into action again. Then, after lot of pushing and pulling, finally a triumphant shout came from outside: 'We're beginning to move.'

After further sloshing and slushing, Murphy, with all his gloomy predictions, finally disappeared around the swan-neck and Mr Crapper triumphantly flushed with pride. Thank you, Mr Crapper.

Changing Seasons

When you live alone, winter can be a daunting
prospect, and with Covid thrown in, the challenge
was even greater. But there is also a warm cosiness
and a 'battening down the hatches'
feeling about winter.
The Danes, who despite extremely short hours of
sunlight and long, long winters, are registered by
the Happiness Research Institute as the happiest
people in the world. They seem to have conquered
the winter problem. Their solution is 'Hygge',
which we are told: 'You don't spell it, you feel it.'
Hygge is all about cuddling up with warmth
and comfort and soft lighting.
Maybe we could learn for the Danes?

Goodbye, Goodbye to Summer

Winter is always a challenge, more so when you live alone because of the long, dark evenings, and I wondered what it would be like during the Covid winter. But having read *The Little Book of Hygge, the Danish Way to Live Well'*, I decided to go Danish. But before that time came and the real winter finally kicked in, it was time to put the garden to bed. The sweet peas had deteriorated from the vibrant rampant climbers of early June into wispy, grey, October ghosts, clinging feebly to their upright obelisks and trellises. Their once green tendrils had lost their grip and like the grey-haired Miss Faversham of *Great Expectations* they were now but wisps and shadows of their former selves. I felt a certain fellow feeling with them, but unfortunately the time for botanical euthanasia had come. They had served me well in filling the summer days with their rainbows of gorgeous colours and heavenly essences, and as an added bonus to that exuberance the more you snip sweet peas to bring their delights indoors the faster they replenish themselves and expand their outdoor display. There are no garden flowers as generous and enchanting as sweet peas, in my opinion. They drench the morning air with their dewy perfume and scent the twilight with their heady aroma. A flower for all times of the day, but now having brought delight to the summer days of 2020 that day alas was done. But I was very grateful to them for their solidarity through the difficult times during which the pandemic held us all in its malevolent gaze. Now, as it again growled in the undergrowth and moved closer, the therapy of putting the garden to bed served the double purpose of keeping me within my own compound, and also busy and focused. No doubt, but a garden is a thing of beauty and a job forever, and a constant source of therapy in the doing.

Next in the firing line for demolition were the poppies and their dried, spindly uprights were collected for the disposal wheelbarrow, and their heads snipped off and dropped into a large glass jar where some of their black seeds escaped out of the heads of muted soft greys and faded ambers. When full of these parched beauties the jar was a picture of faded elegance and I wished that I was Monet, capable of capturing their faded beauty on canvas.

The gladioli and lilies were falling forward like legless drunks and a quick snip with the pruner sorted that out, and into the wheelbarrow went their dead bodies. A good gardener would now have a garden label ready to pop into these cleared pots to identify the now dormant bodies so that come spring, with the garden about to resurrect, it would be easy to identify who or what was about to rise from the dead. But because I am not such a gardener my spring would be full of surprises. That is my excuse for being a less than efficient performer!

At this point, the nasturtiums, with their bad manners and total disregard for boundaries, were still stridently battling on, providing rumbustious colour from the most unlikely corners. Love them or hate them, one has to give nasturtiums credit for sheer grit and 'stickatitability'. They cling in there and succeed in curving their determined, snaky long legs and fingers around every available structure in sight. There were probably a few more flaunting weeks left in these flamboyant ladies so I let them be and, like the brazen, cheeky hussies that they are, they got away with it. Casting their seeds in all directions they would guarantee their continuity to fight another year, thus assuring their longevity. Self-restraint does not feature in their family archives. There was no need to collect their seeds as they are well able to propagate by themselves. Too able, really!

The fading roses were still producing the odd beautiful bloom – thanks to Monty Don, that advocator of dead-heading, I had been an ardent dead-header this summer. And being confined to barracks lent itself to dedicated service. So now I got out an archaic, long-handled pruner inherited from my departed house companion and gardening friend Mrs C. This pruner has a far-reaching, spindly grasp, manipulated by an ancient fraying rope, and is brilliant for stretching up to depleted archtop rose heads to bring them floating earthwards without damaging a close budding baby companion. Old gardeners are full of gardening wisdom and

resourceful tools. But I stopped there. Maybe this climbing rose could still produce a beautiful bloom when all around was bleak and bare? One wonders did such a bloom inspire that haunting song 'The Last Rose of Summer' ... Who knows, but on a bleak December day when venturing out into the garden, such a rose might bring a ray of comfort and hope. So, let that rose be! Sometimes gardens need to be left to their own devices to create little surprises. Charlie Wilkins, who for many years through his weekly column in *The Examiner* nurtured gardening in the most unlikely souls, including mine, always advocated the need for allowing a garden the freedom to do its own thing. Thus could nature nurture little miracles. And in today's climate we all need the joy of little miracles.

But sometimes, to make miracles happen, you have to plant them as well, so while putting the summer garden to bed, ideas of planting for the coming spring began to germinate in my mind. But they needed to be in more than my mind! So I got on to West Cork Bulbs and put in an order for tulips and other spring bulbs, remembering that the previous spring the tulips had saved my sanity when the pandemic struck without warning in March and shot us all suddenly into lockdown. Then the beautiful tulips were my saviours and I was so grateful to them and so glad I had planted dozens of them the previous autumn. Could nature have anticipated our forthcoming dilemma and motivated me to plant? Who knows!

While putting the garden to bed this time another bright

idea germinated: to plant sweat-pea seeds outside for next season. I did this once before and it was a resounding success; the sweet peas over-wintered outside and the following late spring and early summer were off to a flying start. Maybe we had a very mild winter that year, but who knows, it could happen again this year. It was worth a chance! These seeds do not cost a fortune, so the monetary investment is nominal, and the delight of waiting and watching out for their early germinating and growth would be a treat. Much of gardening is about anticipatory visualisation!

The joy of anticipation
Awaiting dreams' realisation
Looking forward is the fun
Of happy things yet to come.

Flower Power

With a slam of brakes a car ground to a halt in front of my window and an irate lady wearing a thunderous expression charged out of it, banging the door so hard behind her that the car shuddered in resistance. As she made a purposeful dash towards the shop next door, she resolutely whipped a large, glossy handbag over her shoulder. Then, suddenly, her eyes fell on the window box full of glowing flowers and her expression miraculously softened. A smile stole across her face. For a few seconds she stood absorbing the flowers and then slowly stooped forwards to smell and tenderly touch them. Her whole demeanour had changed. Flower power.

Maybe window sills are like stages on which window boxes appear like actors, to brighten up our lives and bring a smile to our faces. These window boxes can have two shows, a summer and winter one. The summer flowers add delight to already delightful days, but the winter ones ignite hope and bring light and comfort to drab, dreary days. They nourish our sense of wellbeing and fan the feel-good factor that winter days challenge. We need flowers more in the winter than in the summer. And maybe this winter, with the added fog of Covid blighting our lives, window boxes

were more important than ever.

So this October when the summer window boxes were showing the beginnings of a slow demise, the time had come to ring Willie in the nearby garden centre to enquire about the arrival date of the primulas already ordered for the winter boxes. 'Should be in on the thirteenth of November,' he informed me.

That deadline told me that it was time to bring down the winter window boxes from the top of the garden and prepare them for the arrival of the primulas. These boxes had not been seen since they were abandoned up there last May and now was the time to pay them a visit to see how things were with them. Already sleeping in them were the spring bulbs from previous years, and having cleared the fallen leaves and general debris off one box I noticed that the tiny tips of some bulbs were waking up and attempting a tentative exploratory peep above the soil. It was a delight to see them. After a pretty moist summer these rain-soaked boxes were now weighty boys, requiring male muscle to be moved. The days when I could whip them up and bear them down along the sloping garden paths and stone steps were long gone, so it was time to exercise maternal blackmail by telling the next generation that it was pay-back time.

It may be best make it clear at this stage that we are talking here about quite a lot of window boxes – over twenty – due to the fact that I live on a street corner with windows at the front and sides. So before these boxes arrived down from the top of the garden, tables needed to be erected in the backyard to facilitate ease of planting. Gone are the days of popping up and down like a rubber robot, so out of a back shed were dragged two foldable tables on which was laid a tablecloth of empty compost bags to avoid filial complaints of 'destroying my fine tables with your bloody muddy window boxes'. Once the boxes were all down from the top of the garden and laid out on the tables, a clean-up operation commenced and it was a delight to say hello and welcome the numerous little shoots already breaking through the sodden earth. Having all the boxes cleaned and ready to receive the primulas should make planting day more manageable. I hoped!

As Friday the thirteenth approached I kept a wary eye on the weather forecast and to my delight the forecast for Friday was very good. And it was the only good day that week or the following week. Would my good luck hold? The next lucky break would be if the primulas actually arrived into the garden centre on Friday as scheduled. After a week of wet, grey, dreary days, Friday dawned bright and clear with a long-absent sun making a welcome return – but knowing that he was only on a flying visit, full of apprehensive expectations I rang Willie to be greeted by an amused reaction: 'You must have telepathy. They are just being delivered off the truck.'

'How soon will I have them?' I asked anxiously, thinking of my one precious dry day.

'Within the hour.'

Miracles do happen, I thought gratefully, and just as the Angelus bell up the hill was pealing forth the midday hour I opened the back gate and, as promised, the primulas arrived, thirteen trays, each containing twelve plants. Contrary to belief, thirteen was proving to be a lucky number on Friday the 13th!

Because they had just been delivered to Willie from the grower I mistakenly anticipated that they would be well watered, but not so, not so. Dry as pepper all of them. So, with Monty Don's caution for the need for adequate soaking chiming in my head, the big soak began. Luckily, parked under a drainage shoot at the bottom of the yard was an ancient plastic baby bath full of rainwater, which is much kinder to baby plants than the tap variety. This could encompass two full trays. Then around the yard were other containers also full of rainwater, so into each of these went a number of little pots. The soaking time slowed down progress, and the stooping and rising involved in the process was not kind to muscles long past their flexibility date, but eventually some plants were sufficiently saturated for planting to commence. These plants were gently eased in between the sprouting bulbs, and deeper bulbs not yet having made a breakthrough had to be taken into consideration too. So it was a slow, cautious operation, but thankfully no evil weevil was found lurking in the depths.

Beginning with the downstairs window boxes for the front of the house, I then continued with those for around the side, and as things progressed the sun turned a November day into a June day, and the birds serenaded from surrounding trees – and a wave of wellbeing encompassed me.

It was a great day to be alive and all was well with the world until my aching body protested and demanded a reprieve, and my inner vacuum demanded sustenance. So I headed for the back door, depositing gardening boots on the mat and casting apron and jacket on the floor in transit to the kitchen. I put the kettle on the Aga and collapsed on to the couch feeling that I might never again achieve the perpendicular. However, a steaming kettle signalled resurrection time, and after rising with much audible groaning and moaning, I assembled a salad sandwich and bore the tray outside, collecting *en route* a soft, downy cushion for the garden chair, to enjoy what could be one of the last days of outside dining.

Then, before I might decide that my energy levels were extinct it was time to rise again and I was soon back in action. Gradually all the plants, having had their soak, were finding a home, until finally it was down to the hanging baskets. Then they were done, and with completion came a great sense of achievement. No doubt about it, but there is therapy in doing.

This completed job really warranted a war dance of triumph, but though the spirit was willing the aching body was not quite up to it. But the satisfaction of seeing all the fresh, green plants in location was worth all the aches and pains, and my father's advice to himself came to mind: 'Better to keep moving rather than rust like an old mowing machine in the dyke.'

The next step was to get all the boxes out onto the windows sills, downstairs and upstairs. The upstairs ones were the big challenge because the only route to those sills is to go onto the roof of the back porch and in through a door leading off it. Male muscle was required again. As the six o'clock Angelus bell up the hill again pealed forth, all the boxes were in place. Alleluia!

During the bleak winter months ahead these primulas and bulbs would flower forth and brighten up dull days. The power of flowers.

And Here Comes Christmas

Moss was on my mind. Soft, wispy, downy bundles of abundant gorgeous dry, fluffy moss. And to harvest it, a dry, calm, sunny day. This special moss is available in a secluded, shady, nearby wood where people seldom go. This wood was in my mind's eye, but the special day was in the mind of God, and I would have to wait for a divine decision for such a day to come my way. And then, suddenly, after a queue of grey, wet, foggy, depressing days, this special day came dancing like a swirling ballerina along the horizon and the whole world lit up. Then it was a case of grasp the moment, so I rang a son who might be available.

'Are you busy?' This was the wrong question because what male will admit to not being busy?

'What do you want?'

To which I was tempted to demand: why do men always answer one question with another, but when seeking a favour you choose your words with care as diplomacy is the name of this game.

'Would you like a walk around Shippool wood?' I invited, as enticingly as possible. 'It's such a beautiful day.' I

emphasised the word 'beautiful'.

But this son knows his mother's strategies and went straight to the heart of the matter. 'You're looking for moss,' he told me, but then added, 'Be there in ten minutes.'

This son and his siblings had spent the Sunday afternoons before every Christmas of his childhood exploring Shippool Wood while his mother foraged for moss or anything else conducive to Christmas decorating. Obviously he had not forgotten.

So, after doing a little dance of anticipation around the kitchen, I headed for the back porch and gathered up a couple of ancient timber garden trugs from the top of the corner cupboard. These venerable old boys, collected during years of rooting around musty junk shops, would be the best for the job on hand as the moss could be spread out in layers and the top layer would not suppress the exuberance of the layer beneath. After years of moss gathering I had brought it down to a fine art, but my masked son, on arrival, was not impressed with my assortment of old boys and whipped out a red plastic obscenity from the garden shed, which would undoubtedly hold far more, but then, too many layers of damp moss might flatten those beneath. But did I protest? Certainly not. After years of dealing with the complexity of the male ego I know when to keep my mouth shut, and mask-wearing is certainly conducive to just that. We would probably have a much more silent and compliant world were this mask-wearing to continue indefinitely. Having a conversation while gagged by a mask is conducive to a more careful choice of words, and to get involved in an argument when wearing one defies common sense and logic because should the argument get over-heated one could finish up choking on the mask. So I kept my mouth shut and silently climbed on board, and, with the back seat buried beneath a complexity of containers, we headed for the wood.

Aren't woods wonderful! Shippool Wood is the hidden jewel in the crown of Innishannon. Clinging to a steep hillside along the banks of the Bandon river as it curves its way to Kinsale harbour, the trees in this wood have over the years fallen victim to old age and to this very steep slope. Some have slid downwards, blocking access, so the whole place has got choked and needs rejuvenating and replanting. Unfortunately, when Coillte began a regeneration plan some years previously they were prevented from completing it by some well-meaning but misguided tree huggers, and so now a large part of this wonderful wood is no longer accessible to the public because of safety issues. But for wildlife and moss gatherers it is a hidden haven.

When we arrived in the wood we headed off in different directions so I pocketed my mask and appreciatively breathed in the woody air and viewed the tranquil swans sail majestically along the river in the valley down below. The smell of a wood defies analysis and my verbal capabilities, but once absorbed this smell is never forgotten, and it reawakens and dances along the paths with you as you enter any wood. Along the paths, layers of multi-coloured leaves whisper beneath your feet and ancient trees wrapped in soft, green lichen coats creeping down to their long, sinewy toes, grip the banks along either side of you.

But in here you are not alone and when you stand absolutely still you can hear the wood breathe and sense the sound of all the little creatures hidden in its silent depths. For many years I have harboured a secret dream of one night sleeping in this wood, listening to the sounds of the night, and waking up in the morning to the music of the dawn chorus. It has never happened, but who knows in another life I may come back as one of our feathered friends and be part of that dawn chorus.

But in the meantime into my silent haven trickled the sound of water and it was only then that the waterfall up ahead was remembered. In summer it is a trickle, but now in mid-winter it was a cascade of water tumbling down over black, glistening rocks and pushing itself around fallen tree trunks on its hurried way down to the river below. Spanning it is a little wooded bridge from where you can look upwards at the cascading water and follow it down as it dances its way beneath you and onwards in a swirl of foam into the waiting Bandon river to be carried along into the open mouth of Kinsale harbour.

Suddenly from the top of the waterfall a voice floated down. 'Where's your moss?' My masked chauffeur displayed his red container overflowing with moss.

'Take off your mask, we're miles apart and the trees will hardly give us Covid – and breathe in God's air,' I advised him.

'This is a wood,' he informed me, 'not a health farm.'

'Did you never hear of forest bathing?'

'No,' he asserted, 'anyway we're here for moss not for a bath.'

So I made my way to the remnants of a little ruin which many moons earlier may have been a wood-cutter's cabin but is now a crumbling collection of old stones, and applied myself to the job on hand —and, oh boys, was there a profusion of the most wonderful moss here! Having eased off the fluffy layers I shook them gingerly, hoping to encourage the little creatures inside to scurry out and find other shelter before they were laid in the trugs and taken home with me. I felt like a marauding Viking invader, but I was trying to reduce the impact of my intrusion into their world.

On returning to the bridge with laden trugs, I found a camera-happy son capturing the waterfall and dispatching it to a brother travel-restricted in another country. Immediately an envious return message arrived: 'Ye're in Shippool Wood.' The wonder of modern communications – sometimes over-intrusive but in this time of Covid a wonderful means of connection.

Back home, the trugs full of moss were laid out around the back porch which they filled with their musky, woody smell. The first step into getting ready for Christmas had been taken.

The second step towards Christmas was selecting the Christmas tree, which was initiated by seven-year-old Ellie, whose Christmas decorating enthusiasm could no longer be restrained. So the following evening, with her masked mother, brother Tim and masked me on board, we headed for John's Christmas tree display on his farm just outside the village. There we were spoilt for choice as a multitude of trees were arranged on stands all around the large farmyard. Ellie got straight down to business, walking around accessing the merits of each tree, while four-year-old Tim decided that this was the ideal scenario for jumping out suddenly from between the dark trees to give unsuspecting buyers the surprise present of a heart attack for Christmas.

Eventually, with gentle nudging in the desired direction from her mother, their tree was chosen and Ellie then turned her attention to the more pliable me, and, as in Brexit, we too finally reach an agreement. We paid up in the open-fronted shed and shortly after arriving home both trees were delivered.

The delivery lads were too local teenagers and when they landed the tree in the backyard one of them looked around at the large tree-fern and potted plants and said appreciatively, 'Isn't this is a lovely corner!' I was delighted. His grandmother had been a lover of beautiful things; the apple had not fallen far from the tree.

The next step towards Christmas was the long-planned visit to Santa that had to be booked weeks in advance. Hosting Santa in the time of Covid necessitates huge open-air spaces in which to comply with all the necessary health-care specifications. A large farm is the ideal venue, so The Farm in Grenagh was booked and on a Saturday before Christmas

we were about to descend on it.

I was included in the family plan and it was up to me in the present circumstances to weigh up the pros and cons and make my own decision about going. To stay at home would undoubtedly be the safer option but with Covid, I had discovered, it was all about keeping the balance. If you stayed totally devoid of human company you would be physically safe but could get cabin fever in the process. So I did a mental check and decided that as I was in their bubble I would go. Over the years, with children and grandchildren, I have enjoyed – and endured – many visits to Santa. Some best forgotten, some memorable for all the wrong reasons, and others straight out of the *Night before Christmas*. Which would this be?

The Highway to Santa

With a new baby on the way and with her own mother in mind, my daughter had decided some months ago to change her car for a larger model. So, with a supportive husband and a car enthusiast brother in an advisory capacity, my daughter eased herself in and out of a multiplicity of vehicles before the final selection was reached, and a sleek, grey model arrived just before the new baby and thankfully pre-Covid. And in this model, mother and father sit out front, Yours Truly behind with a baby seat for Tim to my right and a baby seat to my left for baby Conor, now almost a year old, and behind, in the boot, an additional seat for Ellie, who absolutely adores her new location. And thereby hangs a tale. Because this back seat is where Tim also wants to be and constantly strives to attain. And he is determined to get there at all costs. Sometimes Ellie, in an effort to placate him or maybe because she knows that it could never really happen, offers to swop seats. The reason that this exchange could never take place is because Tim can be a bad car traveller and a puking session is always a possibility. This would cause absolute consternation as this extra seat is located next to Conor's buggy, family jackets and all the other paraphernalia that are the essential requirements for family outings with three small children on board. And the prospect of all these essentials being baptised in a sea of vomit is simply beyond consideration. So Tim simply cannot be allowed to achieve his objective. But Tim thinks otherwise and is determined to score his goal. Self-help gurus advocate a certain tenacity such that if at first you do not succeed you should try and try again – they would certainly applaud Tim's attitude to life. But not so his fellow travellers. But hopefully on our journey to Santa things might be different. So we would have to wait and see how Tim's body and state of mind would be on that particular day. It could be that we might have a whole new little man. Unlikely, but hope swells eternal in the parental human heart and even more so in the grandparental human heart of a doting Nana.

The departure deadline came and went on the morning, which is no great surprise to me as my daughter, who is called after her grandmother, has also unfortunately inherited one her less desirable characteristics, which is a total inability to be on time. This was a flaw in my mother's otherwise admirable personality that drove my father, who was always ready half an hour ahead of take-off, absolutely crazy. Her granddaughter, however, has no such monitor in her life and the result is that they are constantly running late.

Finally on the Santa morning we all made it to the car and got ourselves arranged. Then I checked that Tim's emergency sick bucket and towel were at the ready. The whole boarding process was similar to embarking on an Aer Lingus flight, even down to the contents of the seat pockets and availability of adult face masks instead of life jackets to encompass all oncoming eventualities. However when Tim's turn to board came he did not comply with Aer Lingus procedures and decided to have a melt down on the tarmac. He demanded a change in the seating arrangements. Unfortunately, or maybe fortunately, there were no airport police to come to the rescue, so this passenger had to be coaxed, cautioned, bribed and finally seduced by a threat that the Big Red Man in waiting would be beyond consolation were he to witness this passenger's behaviour prior to arrival. So as the clock ticked relentlessly towards the prescribed landing time, we were all finally belted in and ready for take-off. Then, as we all settled ourselves down in our respective corners, an announcement came from the cockpit informing us that due to the late take-off time the pilot had no choice but to take a shorter route. Now, on this particular journey, a short cut means narrow backroads with twisty bends, and, worse still, high, hilly inclines which are not conducive to sedate, steady journeying. Undoubtedly there were turbulent times up ahead and Tim was the first passenger on board to succumb to the turbulence.

'I'm tired,' he wailed, which translated meant 'I'm sick', and he wriggled around desperately in his seat endeavouring to find ease from the revolving contents of his stomach. As it was a cold, dry, sunny day we opened all the windows to create an air flow. But with no success. So we tried alternatives of all kinds of distractions, like counting tractors in passing fields to numbering sparkling Christmas trees in roadside windows – but all no good. Despite his love of tractors, Tim could not be distracted from his present agitated condition and he wriggled around desperately as the contents of his stomach strove to exit their present confines. And I was on standby with my plastic sand bucket that was meant for happier occasions. When Tim eventually spewed forth, the perfectly placed bucket was the ideal receptacle to catch the emerging flow. After years of car travel with puking children and grandchildren, I consider myself an expert in this department. But, however smart I may consider myself to be, I was totally unprepared for a distressed wail on my left, alerting me to the fact that there was a further eruption brewing, and I whirled around to behold a colourful waterfall coursing down little Conor's Santa dribbler.

'Towel – fast!' I yelled to his mother and it came flying back over her head. I managed to catch Conor's flow just before it hit his Santa jumper. Alleluia! But this pride in my success was shortlived with the realisation that Tim was not quite finished, and was about to have another eruption. I dived too late to retrieve the bucket being held between my feet on the floor.

'Another towel,' I yelled in desperation and back came one of Conor's emergency clean-up cloths, with which I tried to redeem Tim's Santa jumper. But once Tim's stomach had eased he turned his attention to his appearance, and insisted that a new outfit would be a requirement to meet

Santa. So a comprehensive clean-up had to take place before he was ready to be persuaded that he might be sufficiently presentable to meet the Big Man in Red. When he was satisfied that he was totally smell- and vomit-free, I breathed a thankful sigh of relief – but suddenly from the back seat came a plaintive wail. It was Ellie, 'I'm feeling sick!', which I could well understand because at this stage I was not feeling too good myself.

But then, miraculously, the gates to heaven appeared in front of us. We had landed. Alleluia. We all tumbled headlong out of the car, swallowing gulps of fresh air and grateful at last to be standing on *terra firma*. And we had made it on schedule too, but no one applauded the poor pilot, though we were silently grateful to him that, despite all the odds, he had got us there in time.

Five minutes later the turbulent flight was all forgotten as we were led by a cheery elf to Santa's barn. But when we were ushered into his cave there was no Santa, only an impressive red velvet armchair beside a huge dark fireplace. Then, suddenly, there was a rumble in the chimney and down came a big red boot, followed by another, and a giant Santa emerged out of the fireplace, masked and separated from us by a clear plastic sheet – but because this was now the norm in their lives Ellie and Tim took the plastic separation totally in their stride. Despite Covid and a somewhat stormy start, Santa had woven his magic spell.

The last piece of the Christmas jigsaw was also put in place when, the following day, Ellie decided that I needed

help with the making of the mince pies. So she arrived in the early afternoon and cracked into action.

'Nana, where's my apron?' she demanded.

'Wherever you left it,' I told her.

'Oh, it's up in the art room, since we were painting there!' And she disappeared up the stairs and I listened carefully to her footsteps, fearful that she might continue upwards to the next floor where a Certain Man had parked his goods. However, Ellie is nothing if not focused, and within minutes she was back down dressed for the occasion.

'Now, Nana,' I was instructed as she remembered the drill from last year, 'you make the pastry, I will do the cutting out, the putting in of the mincemeat and the covering. You will put them in the oven and both of us will remember not to let them burn.'

'Right, Ma'am,' I agreed. As we proceeded she got stuck into the job with absolute focus and when we were running in chain-gang precision, her mind moved onto the forthcoming big occasion.

'Nana! Jesus was the son of God,' she stated.

'Right,' I agreed, wondering what was coming down the tracks.

'But Mary was married to Joseph.'

This could get interesting.

'But she stayed married to Joseph.'

'She did,' I agreed. I began to wonder what theological conundrum could be coming my way. But I need not have worried because Ellie had it all figured out.

'That was best,' she declared conclusively, 'because Mary couldn't really have said to Joseph: Joseph, I'm out of here.'

'Certainly not,' I agreed, breathing a sigh of relief.

Releasing Happy Hormones

This year it was quite difficult to take down Christmas. Even though it was a Christmas like no other with no large gatherings, it was still cheerful. But it was Little Christmas Day now, Nollaig na mBan, and tomorrow was the day the decorations should come down. My grandmother termed this 'taking down the Christmas' and we did not do so before 7 January as she told us that prior to this there was an angel sitting on the spike of every holly branch. You did not argue with my grandmother, so we believed her! Then and now in most houses 7 January was the normal taking-down day and usually by then you're glad to clear the clutter. But not this year. Because this year was not normal and we did not want to clear the clutter, did not want to let go of all the comforting trappings of Christmas. Like Trump, I did not want to accept reality but wanted to hang onto Christmas just as he wanted to hold onto the White House. I didn't want to let go. This year we all needed Christmas to comfort us at the end of a long, tough year. And now was the time to say goodbye to all the small comforting little rituals of Christmas.

It was time to say goodbye to coming down the stairs each morning and plugging in the little candles that lit up the crib at the end of the corridor, where some old and battered, but much-loved crib figures were surrounded by a menagerie of animals and birds tucked into driftwood and mountains of moss. This was the first year for these little candles, gifted to me the previous year for the tree, but they did not work well on it as they tilted all over the place. On the driftwood they held their ground and cast a soft glow that was a delight every morning. On the table beneath the window, the rich red frankincense candle brought the essence of the Wise Men alive, while outside that window the garden could be admired in its winter sleep. Next step in the morning ritual was to go into the Seomra Ciúin where there was a much posher crib also waiting to be lit up every morning. This crib was only on loan as it was a wedding gift to my daughter – but her three small children, like King Herod, could capture baby Jesus! So the Wise Men had wisely led the Holy Family into my house for safe-keeping. These are elegant, porcelain figures, needing a much more impressive layout than moss and driftwood. And white is the theme here, sitting on a dark green base. This base is formed from the recycled curtains of an old church confessional that were destined for a skip when the church was being restored. Made of top-quality fabric they covered my deep window sill with a smooth, dark green base. A few weeks before, when setting it up, I held my breath in case of a catastrophe, but all had landed safely. Then for the real test of ingenuity: the day before set-up, with a rush of creative anticipatory visualisation to the head, I had enjoyed an hour out in the yard happily applying white paint to the light, thin branches of an acer tree. The plan was that these branches would arch over the crib and along them would perch little white birds and candles. I held my breath as all these were being carefully manoeuvred into position. The last thing needed was that any delicate figurine should lose a limb. But finally all were safely in place and, breathing a sigh of relief, I went out into the street to view how they looked from outside the window. Pretty good, I felt. Ellie and Tim, and hopefully other children passing by, would enjoy the crib, which was safe from little fingers.

The tables in the front hall were dressed in red robes and the big Teddy Bear Santa on the back of the front door was a picture of cuddlesome warmth. Many years ago he was created by the residents of nearby St Patrick's Upton under the direction of Sr Attracta, now long gone, as is her workshop. But I am glad to have memories of her and her willing helpers. Isn't Christmas full of memories and traditions? How could I bear to take them down? The house would look so empty this year with no visitors allowed.

Then I went into the room holding the Christmas tree, which this year, due to better care, looked as good as the day it was erected. It was lovely at night to sit in here in the glow of this lit tree and view the tall village Christmas tree across the road, and all the other village trees glowing down along the street. Over Christmas the village is always magical and this year we decorated earlier, feeling the need for that extra brightness for ourselves and passing traffic. In the kitchen the tops of the dressers were draped with Christmas cards from friends. This year we were more conscious of the need to keep in touch.

Later that day I decided to go for a walk to clear the head and release happy hormones. Outside, the primulas in the window boxes planted in November were now about to burst into bloom. It would do your heart good do see them. *En route* through the churchyard I called into the church to light a candle and say a prayer. It was good that in this lockdown period the churches were still open and people were constantly in and out. During this lockdown we needed every source of spiritual sustenance available. Outside I stood to admire the life-size crib that every year is reassembled by the two parishioners who made it. Next week they would be back to take it down – or maybe we might leave it for a few more weeks? The graves in the surrounding graveyard showed evidence of Christmas attention too with fresh pots of flowers and cheery holly wreaths. Always at Christmas, people remembered their departed loved ones and regularly over Christmas visited their family graves. In our own plot the daffodils and snowdrops were peeping above the ground and the defiant yellow marigolds that should have packed their bags and been long gone, were still hanging gallantly in there. By the rear entrance beside the pathway into Bothar as Sop, a magnificent magnolia that annually bursts into gorgeous blooms before all others was already silently plumping up her soft buds, full of promise. When she blossomed she would be a soft, white, voluptuous, breath-taking sight, lighting up all our lives. I think I might have gathered the energy and courage now to actually take down Christmas.

Baby, It's Cold Outside

With the cosiness of Christmas lights and decorations gone, I decided that it might be nice, like the Danes, to surround myself with woolly cosiness instead. But I was not the only one thinking of covering up! The canine world was one jump ahead of me.

Dogs must be delighted with Covid because they were being exercised to their limits, but even the most exuberant of them surely had to be reaching exercise saturation point. Our roads were now lined with a multiplicity of dogs and walkers of all shapes and sizes, and there were some rather unusual combinations. You might see a very large man purposefully leading forward tiny bundles of fluff at the end of rather impressive lethal leather leads, such as a farmer might use to drag a reluctant bull through a muddy gap. Then you could encounter a dainty lady being dragged along by a masterful mastiff. Some walkers had their charges togged out for this extremely cold weather, with some miniature dogs immersed in fur jackets, making it difficult to determine where the jacket ended and the dog began. When, many years ago, I first encountered doggy wear in a New

York pet shop I was mesmerised, but where America leads we follow. Being a farmer's daughter, where dogs were for rounding up cattle or keeping unwelcome intruders at bay, the idea of dressing up of dogs in fancy gear always brought a smile to my face. But now that smile had been wiped off. The temperature had plummeted and my mid-thigh jacket, which my father would have scornfully termed 'a bum freezer', was totally inadequate – then along would come a happy doggy wrapped up from ears to tail in pink fur – and I thought 'you lucky lady'.

But this little bundle of pink warmth brought home to me that the time had come for me too to cover my own extremities and bring forth the Galway shawl. This was the mother of all greatcoats. I think of my '*cóta mór*' in the feminine because when you don her you are encompassed in the arms of a warm, maternal embrace. This ankle-length, pure wool blanket of comfort was purchased in Galway over thirty years ago and has escaped many a decluttering foray, though she sailed very close to the wind when Marie Kondo swooped in like a hovering hawk and the whole house got the deepest deep clean that it had ever experienced. But Marie Kondo was no match for the Galway girl, and the woman from the West of Ireland survived the contest, holding her ground and refusing to be outwitted by the Japanese goddess of decluttering. But what finally shot the winning Galway goal into the Marie Kondo net was the memory of past successes when tough conditions prevailed. So now, whenever sub-zero levels return, out comes the Galway shawl to combat them. And as we shivered in the arctic conditions of 2021 winter, how glad was I of that Galway win! Already crippled by the pandemic, the freezing winter conditions were almost a step too far for me, but the Galway shawl saved the day.

Sometimes the circumstances in which you buy something forever colour your relationship with it. When I don my Galway shawl, it wings me back to a golden autumn day in Galway city. At the time the city was not cordoned off by a mesmerising network of roundabouts, so we simply drove right into Eyre Square in the middle of the city and parked practically on the lap of Pádraic Ó Conaire, that irresistible little man, who, because everyone wanted to hug his memorial statue, had to be removed for his own safety. Then a ramble along the colourful streets to do a book signing in Kenny's, where the wonderful Mrs Kenny's warm personality flowed over her beehive of books, and browsers turned every visit into a memory to be forever treasured. Later that day, traversing the intriguing streets of historic Galway, which still held the flavour of an old market town, we eventually wandered into Moon's department store where the Galway shawl was lying in wait. Though slightly overawed by its copious flowing capacity, the final decision to purchase was fast-forwarded by a convincing Galway shop assistant and a husband, who, like my mother, believed that warmth was more important than style. A case of forget the look, feel the quality.

So we came home with what over the years I lovingly

refer to as my Galway shawl, which, when the temperatures plunge, wraps me in its warm, loving arms, and engulfs me too in so many memories. And now, with Covid numbers soaring high and temperatures plummeting, I was very appreciative of my Galway shawl.

But when the cold seeps into the bone-marrow most women of my vintage have old faithfuls buried at the bottom of our drawers that we gratefully dig out to rescue us from freezing to death. My second *aide-de-camp*, when icicles glisten, is my Ballybunion blanket, which is actually older than the Galway shawl. On that purchasing occasion, it was my mother who was the consultant – she, who would run a knowing hand along any potential acquisition to make an astute assessment of its weave and potential durability. At the time in Ballybunion was Ballybunion Knitwear, wisely located beside the church to which most people on holiday at the time invariably found their way. Before arriving at the church you came on the knitwear shop surrounded by a garden overflowing with an abundance of the most glorious roses. Immersed in the scent of roses, you stood entranced in front of impressive elegant windows viewing sleek mannekins in fine tweeds and gorgeous knitwear, surrounded by sparkling crystal. So after calling to the house of God, you returned to that basilica of style where even the angels could be tempted.

One evening after a pleasurable perusal along the shelves I came across a temptation beyond all resistance. A part-woven and part-knit, gorgeous, rich red pure wool jumper.

The sleeves were woven and the body an intricate complexity of Aran and double-knit layers. Its gorgeous texture was an intoxication to the senses. The woman who created this irresistible, luxurious masterpiece had to be a genius – for some reason I assumed it was a woman. Now, I will admit to wincing a little at the price, but my mother, who was certainly not into big spending, swished that impediment aside, working on the principle that long after you have forgotten the price you remember the quality. And so home with me came the Ballybunion blanket and now, over thirty years later, the price is indeed long forgotten but the quality lingers on.

Now, if in a cold spell you have an outer layer of a Galway shawl and inside it a body layer of a Ballybunion blanket, you then need a layer for the lower regions and achieving this in today's world is no small challenge. Because where can you go to buy warm knickers? Certainly not into our trendy lingerie boutiques. Our grandmothers had no such problem. My grandmother had the biggest, warmest, pink knickers you could ever imagine. They also came in navy blue and the material for their creation was interlock, a word which Google defines as 'architectural ironmongery', which certainly gives food for thought. Obviously, Google did not have a grandmother with an interlock knickers. Into it my grandmother tucked the tails of numerous vests and petticoats and was then ready to visit the Antarctic.

But those roomy draper's shops that fulfilled all these requirements are long gone. The one in our town was packed ceiling high with huge rolls of material, hanks of knitting wool, little chests of colourful reels of thread, boots and shoes for all ages and could adequately tog out its customers from toddlers to centenarians, and dress you for Holy Communion, Confirmation, Weddings and even for your final farewell.

All these draper's shops, however, have disappeared. Once recently, while on a visit to Dingle and romancing to a friend who lived there about their wonderful craft and gift shops, I was told firmly, 'That's fine for visitors but you couldn't buy a knickers in Dingle.' Which is probably true of most towns in Ireland now. But there is one such shop left! Tucked away in a small town on the Cork-Kerry border is a little rabbit warren of a shop that stocks a multitude of all kinds of everything, including lovely warm knickers. Not as ample as my grandmother's, but adequate to requirements. By the time Covid has departed we may have discovered much about the hidden secrets of rural Ireland.

Over a warm knickers has to go a garment of equal warmth, and sleeping at the back of my wardrobe for many years is such a treasure, discovered in an Aladdin's cave in Kenmare many years ago where a wonderful woman designed and wove highly fashionable pure wool garments. Designed to last and look good for all occasions, my black wool pants is an insulation for the lower regions and whenever it is brought forth I whisper in gratitude, 'Thank you, Bren-Mar Jon.'

Now, having covered daywear for sub-zero temperatures, it

was time to think about the far more sublime subject of night-wear. For many years I have been an advocate of Victorian-style long white cotton, lace-trimmed nightdresses, first discovered in a charity shop in Tenterden, in England, while visiting a sister in Kent. This nightdress was a highly desirable replacement for my mother's unromantic, unimaginative interlock passion-crusher. Probably as a result of having been reared with *Little Women* and *Anne of Green Gables*, it was love at first sight when I saw this gorgeous night apparel. A love affair that was to last a lifetime. But recently the present crop of nightdresses had worn dangerously thin and become frazzled at the edges with the bits of lace floating at half-mast. But it was not possible during lockdown to issue forth to buy replacements. There was no such craft shop within the five kilometre travel zone and I do not think that the Gardaí at the checkpoint at the end of our village would be overly impressed with this specific need to travel further afield. And, anyway, craft shops were closed!

Now, at this point I had to admit that nestling in the back of my hot press for many years were some of those extremely warm, comfortable nightdresses gifted by a practical sister, but these had been whipped away in the claws of Marie Kondo. With chilly night temperatures penetrating my threadbare cotton and their trailing bits of lace in danger of tripping me up, the time had come to seek warmer night shelter. I rang the practical sister requesting a parcel in the post with two of her sensible nightdresses. There was no way that she would have fallen victim to Marie Kondo, and it was time for me to swallow my pride, come clean, bite the bullet and confess what I had done. 'You deserve to freeze,' she told me, 'but they'll be in the post.'

Hope Springs Eternal

Two men looked out from prison bars,
One saw the mud, the other saw stars

My strategy to keep focused on the stars is a daily walk. But one January morning before setting out on that walk the little waste bin parked under the kitchen sink had to be emptied. It was filled to capacity as the path to the garden compost bin had been a skating rink for a week, so in the interest of health and safety I'd had to put up with the smelly bin. Now, I grasped it by the handle and headed for the back door.

On opening the door I gasped in awe. Outside was a bright new world. Overnight everything had changed dramatically. There was a clearer light and you could breathe in a softer air. Spring had peeped in to pay us a visit. The devastation of winter was still all around the backyard: the brown skirts of the once elegant cannas were now lying in a mushy mess around their ankles, and the tall, regal dahlia, who had stood upright a few weeks ago, was now in tattered rags after the hard frost. The ferns spraying out of pots around the yard were a sad mat of foxy strands. Not an inspiring sight. But all around them was this new light.

At first I stepped gingerly onto the yard in case some of the black ice was still lying treacherously in wait. But no. Breathing a sigh of relief, I headed straight for the garden gate to the bin to dump the bag I'd brought. But at the entrance I came to a standstill. Right there in front of me, smiling out from beneath a sheltering, dark green shrub, was a cluster of gorgeous, pure white snowdrops. I went straight over to pay homage. Each year the surprise arrival of the first snowdrops is a mini miracle. And, oh boys, did we need miracles this year! For some reason, unlike other flowers, you seldom witness the arrival of snowdrops. One day they seem to appear suddenly in their entirety, almost as if they arrive in full flower – or is it that the weather in which they arrive is often so brutal that we are not around to witness their coming? Then one morning, just like now, there they are, having stolen in while we were indoors keeping ourselves warm. What a delight it was to see them. These delicate, gentle little beauties glowed pristine white in the dark brown desolation of winter.

And they triggered off a voyage of exploration around the garden that I had not seen for over a week because of bad weather. Could there be more snowdrops hiding in remote corners? And indeed there were, some struggling to peep above the overlying gunk of winter debris. I almost heard them utter a grateful sigh of relief as a little patch of earth was cleared around them. Now they could breathe. Then their neighbouring hellebores grabbed my attention, these shy ladies with their drooping heads, hiding beneath their wide umbrella-like hats. Some of the giant leaves were black and mottled, and so a quick return to the back porch to collect a pruner and bucket, and these obliterating leaves were consigned to the bucket. Then these grateful hellebores raised their gentle heads in appreciation and their unimpeded beauty shone forth. Like the snowdrops, their pristine clarity glowed against the dark, sodden winter earth.

Working along the path I came upon Our Lady, lying prone on the ground totally enshrouded in a blue plastic bag. No, she had not fallen from her perch on top of a tree trunk, but a few weeks earlier stormy weather was forecast, so, fearful for her safety, I had eased her off her plinth and slipped the bag down around her to keep the weather at bay. I should have got her into the safety of the back porch, but it was late that night and I feared that we might come a cropper along the slippery slope of the garden. Now in broad daylight it was much safer to rescue her. Ideally, male muscle was still needed, but this was lockdown and there was only me. I tried lifting her, but for some reason she seemed to have got heavier than she had been in the summer.

I looked around for my wheelbarrow, but not a trace of it. That is the problem with living on the same hill as your offspring – whenever you need some specific garden tool it has disappeared. With apologies to my sacred companion, I swore under my breath and decided to go in search of a trolley from the back door of the shop next door. There were actually three of them, so I was spoilt for choice; however, one was too wide for the garden path and another too narrow to hold my passenger, but the remaining one should do the job. I began to wheel it towards the garden gate only to discover that one wheel was punctured. Typical!

I went back up to where Mary was resting and looked across at Joseph, thinking that maybe Ellie's earlier pronouncement still applied: maybe now was not the time for myself and Mary to tell Joseph, 'Joseph, we're out of here.' In the process we might both have a crash landing. So, Mary was tucked in firmly behind a garden seat until the time came when male muscle could be safely summoned. Then she would be brought safely into the back porch where a complete make-over was planned.

Then I turned my attention to Joseph, cutting back the bare-branched rambling roses that were threatening to choke him, and when the faded crocosmia at his feet were cleared I found new shoots sprouting up all around him. The cheery daffodils were beginning to appear along his bank too and my old friendly enemies, the bluebells, were letting me know that they would be here later. This year I was actually delighted to welcome them back, even if they are marauders. Covid had certainly put garden manners on me. The little pink blossoms of the Jacqueline Postill and the understated sarcococca were filling the air with their heavenly scents, and around the garden the birds flitting from branch to branch were singing with anticipation.

They too sensed that spring was on the way. On inspecting their feeders, I realised that many needed a refill, so I did the needful. It was fair exchange: they entertain and I sustain. Then suddenly I heard the sound of flapping wings. The blackbird was back, attacking his imaginary rival in the mirror while his proud partner looked down from her high perch. Nest building was about to begin.

Finally, before leaving the garden, I emptied the kitchen waste into the compost bin where I gathered up some of the collar of composting worms along the rim and cast them inside to get on with the job. Then I headed back down into the yard where the dilapidated cannas got a short back-and-sides and were pushed into a more shaded corner, and then the drooping dahlias were cut back to base. I was delighted to see that the sweet peas, planted in October to give them a head start, had survived the frost, and should now continue to make it to early flowering. The graceful tree fern, the prima donna of the backyard, had thankfully survived the harsh weather, and it was lovely to run your hands along her friendly fronds. I was so happy to see the profusion of bulbs planted in the pots around the yard last October and November now beginning to appear. Last March, when Covid first struck, I had learned the value of these bulbs: back then the bright red and yellow tulips had kept me sane. Little did we think that we would still be in the same boat this year. Maybe just as well we didn't know.

Now, standing at the back door, I felt much easier than

I had on coming out hours earlier, and I began to tick the 'hope' boxes in my head. Covid was still with us, but there were vaccines on the horizon. Spring was on the way and beyond the bars of lockdown, stars were beginning to appear in the sky.

And tomorrow is another day.

Roots

When I go home
I walk the fields,
The quiet fields
Where the warm dew
Had squelched between
My childish toes.
To sit beneath
The cool oak and ash
That sheltered
My adolescent dreams.
These trees stand
With leafy arms
Outstretched
Like a lover's,
Not in passion
But with gentle sighs
Sighs of contentment.
I watch the cows
Graze peaceful
Beside the river
Curving its way
Through furze inches

Into the woods beyond.
This is a holy place
Where men have worked
Close to God's earth
Under the quiet heavens.

Hanging on the walls of all our minds are pictures into which we regularly disappear. Children do it all the time and so do emigrants, as I discovered when book-signing abroad after the publication of *To School through the Fields*. The pictures of their childhood had remained etched in their memories and my writing was simply a conduit back into their own world. During the first cocooning many of us escaped into these pictures, with plans to go home as soon as the travel limit was eased. My picture was the view from the gate of the home place.

It is an ordinary farm gate with no affectations of grandeur and inside it is the passageway leading down to the house. This passage is not impressive enough to be called an avenue, and too wide to be called a boreen, and so was christened the passage, long, long before my time. The Old Road climbs steadily upwards from the local town until it arrives at the gate of our passage, and having reached this summit then curves westwards on an even keel into Kerry. Prior to modern road maintenance, the Old Road got regular face-lifts from the road men who sat along its grassy dykes with an iron hammer and chisel, splitting large rocks into manageable chippings, then tossing them into horse-drawn butts to fill holes from, and so prevent this hilly road reverting to nature. The traffic on this road in my childhood was mainly of the horse and cow variety, with an occasional car. These roadmen lived along the road in cottages provided by the County Council, which in today's world would be termed 'staff accommodation'. Off the road, down long avenues, passages or boreens – the title depending on the quality of the entrance or the self-perceived image of the family in question – lived the farming community.

Our passage was a meandering slope leading from the gate off the Old Road down into our farmyard. Originally this passage could well be compared to the 'rocky road to Dublin', but my father drew horse-and-butt loads of gravelly, mud-encrusted 'pencil stones' from a deep quarry in one of the adjacent fields and tipped them out along its rutted surface. Then he spread the mixture with a shovel and settled it into place with a heavy yard-brush. With the passage of time, the rain washed the mud and loose gravel down between the larger gravel and pencil, and this eventually settled it. Occasionally, if too much rain came and the surface got muddied, he gave it a top-up with more pencil, until finally the entire mass settled down into hard core and became rock solid, and looked after itself. The passage had secured its own future.

When you open the gate off the road into the passage your eyes are magnetically drawn to the breathtaking view spread out in front of you. A patchwork quilt of farm fields, reflecting the seasons, rolls away into the distant Mushera and Clara mountains, sheltered from behind by the arms of the encircling Kerry range. In our day the passage was banked on either side by two high, ferny ditches, topped with blackthorn trees and wild honeysuckle. Between them you were enfolded in silence and absorbed into a sensory feast, within the gentle rustling of bird and bee activity. Behind these high ditches the passage was flanked on either side by farm fields individualised by name: the Brake, which, due to its high, sunny location and rich dark loam, grew the harvest and was the bread-basket of the farm; the Big Hay Seed, a grazing field full of clover and wildflower grasses beloved of the cows; and the Quarry Field, from where gravel was sourced to create farm paths and to dry up muddy gaps between fields.

Due to the need to keep each field and animal activity separate, this passage was intercepted by seven gates on its way from the road down to the house. These were long, iron farm-gates, swinging off solid stone piers, and these gates made ideal perches from the top of which you could view the changing scenes as you made your way down to the house. These gate tops provided the setting for silent viewing or for shared conversation, depending on the circumstances. On a clear day you could watch the changing face of the mountains across the valley and the activities on the farms on the hills nearer home.

At the end of the passage was a sprawling farmyard of cow stalls, stables, hen houses, piggeries, barns and other sheds, galvanised or slated, all used for housing the mis-cellaneous animals of mixed farming. As well as housing the farm fowl and animals, the roofs of these sheds and barns provided shelter for a multiplicity of birds, including owls, whose choice of residence was the stable above the horses' heads. In the centre of this menagerie of animal activity was the farmhouse, from where the needs of all these animals were met as they, in return, provided the farm income. As we were surrounded by groves of trees and a wooded fort, the dawn chorus began the day and the corncrake serenaded late into the night. But of all the birds, it was the curlew, which my father called the Gabaí-rín Rua, with its plaintive call (like the insistent call of a baby goat) that was the most memorable, though the first magical call of the cuckoo was the one more eagerly awaited by us children. But prior to the cuckoo's arrival, swirls of swallows swept in to reclaim their ancestral nests along the cobweb-draped rafters above the cud-chewing cows and snorting horses. Rabbits were in abundance and foxes regularly raided, but it was the hare, who kept a very low profile, that we all wanted to catch sight of.

One of my sisters, who had emigrated in her early twen-ties, sent me this poem years later. These were the pictures hanging in her mind:

Lisdangan
Mist slowly lifts and shadows drift
Pictures come into view,

A rose-washed house in dark green groves,
Places and things I knew.
An ancient fort where Herons nest
A glen where Curlews call,
A Fairy Well where moonbeams dance
Beside a Ferny Wall.
Old woods of Larch and Pine
A river cool and deep,
Where Otters sleep and Salmon leap
And the Poacher waits his time.

Where children walked
Through fields to school
Painting pictures in the dew,
Where the shady lazy Cuckoo calls
All the summer through.
Where the Tawny Owl glides slowly down
And hovers in the Pines,
Where the Vixen call by the Stable wall
Sends shivers down the spine.
Where the Rooster's call
Heralds in the dawn
Where the dewdrops kiss the day.
Then the mists and shadows slowly drift
And the picture fades away.

Mary Frances Taylor Reese

Once when a stranger happened to find his way down along

this meandering passage into our yard he asked my father in wonder, 'Does Almighty God know that people actually live down here?' He probably did, and we grew up very aware of our dependence on Him and on nature in a world where both were all around us.

And so during the long weeks of cocooning and further weeks of isolation through the year my memory chains began to rattle and a dream surfaced that as soon as a gap appeared I would go back to the home place, which was my original cocoon. Time moves on bringing many changes, but memories of our special places remain forever etched within us. This is common to many of us. In my guest-house days a wonderful English lady who, with her husband, ran a large bus company in Sheffield, came every year for a visit. During her stay she simply pottered around the village, walking the woods and along by the river and chatting to old neighbours in the local pubs. One night we went for a walk and sat on a seat by the Bandon river. She told me that for her Innishannon was the place that beckoned when life was proving too much for her. A visit back to Innishannon restored her equilibrium. As a child she had lived here with cousins who had a beautiful old house at the end of the village. They sold up and moved back to London, but Innishannon had remained for her a place of inner restoration for the rest of her life. Maybe we all have special places that beckon when life tests our stamina. And so, when the time came, back I went to my original cocoon.

The view from the gate had not changed. Mountains do not move. I leant on the gate and feasted my eyes on the old familiar landscape. Leaning on this gate and absorbing the world inside it was a wonderful anecdote to the stresses of previous weeks. I eased back the bolt and slowly swung open the long, low gate. And, as always, the view soothed my soul. It is an opening into a world of monastic peace. The stress of the pandemic faded away and for one full day the world of the virus and economic confusion remained outside this gate. Escapism! No doubt about it! But in today's world it's a case of 'whatever it takes', as long as we follow the advice of Lady Windermere 'not to frighten the horses'. And after one calm, sunny day meandering around the fields and over ditches, I came home restored.

When I am drained within
And the light
Which leads me on
Is quenched,
I come to this place
To be healed:
Its serene depths
Reach out to me
In a warm embrace
And I know
That I have come back
To my own place.

Tea for One

I have lived my life
Far from here
But I have taken
This little place
In the walled garden
Of my heart
To rekindle my tranquility.
And when my life spring
Begins to fade
I make a pilgrimage
Back to my own place.

Afterword

Togetherness
No man is an island
Entire of itself,
Every man is a piece of the continent,
A part of the main;
If a clod be washed away by the sea,
Europe is the less.
As well as if a promontory were.
As well as if a manor of thy friend's
Or of thine own were:
Any man's death diminishes me,
Because I am involved in mankind,
And therefore never send to know for whom
  the bell tolls;
It tolls for thee.

When I first read this John Donne poem it took me some time to fully appreciate its depths. But the last two lines stayed with me and sometimes on hearing the church bell toll as I walk up the hill beside my house to a neighbour's funeral, these lines come to mind and I have to marvel at the wisdom and encompassing vision of the poet. John Donne sees us all as part of a larger living entity. Part of the land on which we walk and of the branches of our family tree, attached to the trees of other tribes. Like the woodlands, we share a natural human eco-system. Trees live in the shelter of each other and so do we. Goodness and kindness are the soil enrichers that keep us all well and healthy. Cutting ourselves off from our family or our extended community depletes us. Our family and community, like the earth, returns to us what we put into it, in the process stimulating and enriching us. We are part of the environmental wellbeing of the universe and those who work the land or anyone who contributes to the plant and bee life of the earth brings blessings on us all. Doing the opposite lessens us and those with whom we share the uni-verse. Then we become an island. Should we allow this to happen we grow inward-looking and focused only on our own little domain where each hillock can then become a mountain. Being part of a wider circle stimulates and ener-gises us to delve deeper into our own inner resources.

Maybe lockdown and growing old have much in common as in both we are fire-fighting, the first in a conflagration and the latter in a slow burn. Neither takes place in isolation as both are part of a bigger universe. In the pandemic, the individual behaviour affects the whole community, while in old age the behaviour of the whole community affects the individual. In each experience we become aware of our interdependence and the need to treat others and the earth with loving kindness. John Donne's poem is applicable in both situations. No man is an island.

Kept apart by busy days
We who belong together
As the interlaced fingers
Of praying hands,
Join again in quiet times
At peace in our
Togetherness.